T0013486

Been There, Ate That

A Candy-Coated Childhood

Jules Torti

Pottersfield Press, Lawrencetown Beach,
Nova Scotia, Canada

Copyright © Jules Torti 2022

All rights reserved. No part of this publication may be reproduced or used or stored in any form or by any means – graphic, electronic or mechanical, including photocopying – or by any information storage or retrieval system without the prior written permission of the publisher. Any requests for photocopying, recording, taping or information storage and retrieval systems shall be directed in writing to the publisher or to Access Copyright, The Canadian Copyright Licensing Agency (www.AccessCopyright.ca). This also applies to classroom use.

Library and Archives Canada Cataloguing in Publication

Title: Been there, ate that : a candy-coated childhood / Jules Torti.
Names: Torti, Jules, 1974- author.
Identifiers: Canadiana (print) 20210351675 | Canadiana (ebook) 20210351810 | ISBN 9781989725771 (softcover) | ISBN 9781989725788 (PDF)
Subjects: LCSH: Torti, Jules, 1974—Childhood and youth. | LCSH: Junk food—Humor.
Classification: LCC TX370 .T67 2022 | DDC 641.3002/07—dc23

Cover image: Pamela Detlor

Cover design: Gail LeBlanc

Pottersfield Press gratefully acknowledges the financial support of the Government of Canada for our publishing activities through the Canada Book Fund. We also acknowledge the support of the Canada Council for the Arts and the Province of Nova Scotia which has assisted us to develop and promote our creative industries for the benefit of all Nova Scotians.

Pottersfield Press
248 Leslie Road
East Lawrencetown, Nova Scotia, Canada, B2Z 1T4
Website: www.pottersfieldpress.com
To order, phone 1-800-NIMBUS9 (1-800-646-2879) www.nimbus.ns.ca

Printed in Canada

To everyone who has invited me to their table for something to eat. Thank you.

From the cafeteria ladies at my high school (that gravy!), to my legendary grandmothers, mother (and brother!) – your talents in the kitchen were/are always appreciated, admired and devoured.

Contents

The 1980s

Fish Eyes and Fried Smelts

"Who wants fish eyes?"

My kid sister's face would turn boiled lobster red before the tears spurted from her eyes and the wail began. I swear my great-grandmother did it on purpose, just to get a rise out of Kiley. My sister was reliable for pouts, crossed eyes (for extended periods), wails and general looks of complete disgust. Offering fish eyes was a no-brainer. My brother Dax and I encouraged the crying fits further by opening our mouths and wagging our tongues full of fish eyes in Kiley's direction.

Grandma was accustomed to prepping lunch for a dozen farmhands so feeding the three of us was a genuine piece of cake. Though, she rarely baked cakes. I wouldn't draw a comparison to Nigella or the Barefoot Contessa, but Grandma held her ground and achieved what many wouldn't dare attempt.

Somehow, she had us requesting the likes of fried smelts and slop (a cast iron pan fry-up of beef, onions and peas seasoned only with salt). What kind of kids voluntarily eat that stuff? I mean, it was 1984, not 1884. Grandma lived directly beside us in country terms, just across the train tracks. We made a mad dash from the school bus to her house for two delicious years when both my parents worked late. Her kitchen skills were underappreciated by our unevolved palates. What's trending now is what my grandmother's mainstay was – scratch cooking and food security.

My great-grandmother had just as many wrinkles as a Shar-Pei from a lifetime of sun and cigarettes. Don't be misled – she was not lying supine in the summer exhaling Virginia Slims. Far from it. She was sturdy and sinewy from working in the tobacco fields, her spine bent like a question mark. Her boobs didn't meet the waistline of her polyester pants like most women her age because she was still cutting grass with a scythe and hand-hoeing nearly a half acre of vegetable gardens. She had a permanent seam of dirt under her nails which meant we didn't have to scour our hands raw for inspection as we did for our grandmother in the city.

How Grandma convinced us to sway from our junk food default setting was a pure miracle. The '80s were defined by McCain fries, Captain High Liner fish sticks, food dye Yellow 5, Red 40 and a whole lotta corn syrup. Her "fish eyes" (tapioca pudding in disguise) were homemade and her labour-intensive elderberry pie was a far cry from the McDonald's hot apple pie pockets with molten lava filling.

My age ten diary (circa 1984) showcases all of the above (and more) in great detail. A day's highlight (and full-page entry) was easily dedicated to a Kentucky Fried Chicken one-piece snack meal with potato salad so lubricated with mayo, it could have doubled (and remained intact) as a snowball. These diary entries were recently revealed/leaked to my parents ("friedchickengate") and though the content is thirty-six years old, my dad still caught a little flack for all the KFC stops I had lovingly documented, unbeknownst to my mom who was, no doubt, at home making us a proper dinner. To this day my mother is quite certain I was trying to outdo my classmates and all my diary fast food coverage was fictional. Was it?

Dear diary ... was I a big fat liar?

Like golden retrievers, my sibs and I needed big rewards for positive, co-operative behaviour. We were a difficult, yawning bunch, especially when it involved a full Saturday morning of errands with my dad. Ugh. Canadian Tire. Haircut at Caesar's. Credit Union. It was a boring and familiar lineup that was only made possible with the promise of a reward. That trickery involved KFC if the last stop was Caesar's (as his barbershop was adjacent) or George's for a box of chip wagon fries so greasy you could oil a rusty bike chain. Kiley and I would actually suck on the bottom of the empty box, extracting every bit of salt, vinegar and grease like vultures picking at roadkill. "Those boxes are made out of horse hooves," my mother taunted us. It didn't stop our sucking – we'd rip another strip from the box and spit our dry cardboard balls into the plastic fry bag, unnerved.

If we were in West Brant, fries were often skipped in favour of a pizza bun stuffed with green olives and mushrooms from Gigi's. They were almost as good as the horse hoof fry boxes.

Disclaimer: To ensure that my mother doesn't poison my tiramisu in the near future, she did ensure that we dutifully prescribed to the Canada Food Guide. Trust me, we ate our fair share of carrots, peas and the odd lima bean. Despite barred teeth resistance, Mom trumped our loose interpretations of the Guide, which included Oreo cookies as protein and sour cream and onion chips as a dairy substitute.

Fish eyes was merely the beginning of it all. An *amuse-bouche* if you will.

How to Eat Fried Worms
and Mexican Hats

Hands-down, my spark book was *How to Eat Fried Worms* by Thomas Rockwell. In 2006, thirty-three years after it was first published in 1973, it was adapted into a major motion picture. I can't bring myself to watch it for fear that it will sour my feelings about this triumphant novel.

The plot revolves around four bored boys, a spontaneous bet involving worms, fifty bucks and George Cunningham's brother's minibike. Alan challenged Billy to eat a worm every day for fifteen days straight: "boiled, stewed, fried or fricasseed" was permitted. Alan and his side-kicks, Joe and Tom, provided the wiggly worms and witnesses had to be present at each "meal."

I appreciated Billy's careful consideration of condiments: maple syrup, horseradish, cinnamon sugar, cheese, Worcestershire, mustard and ketchup. He set his orange crate table with jars of maraschinos and piccalilli, as though it were a regular ploughman's lunch. Rockwell managed to make the worm recipes ravishing instead of revolting, even though Billy's first python-sized night crawler entrée was "as big as a souvenir pencil from the Empire State Building."

Billy devoured toasted cheese and worm sandwiches and worms rolled in cornmeal like trout with snips of parsley and a squeeze of lemon. When Mrs. Forrester (Billy's mom) became involved, the recipes were elevated to the likes of "Alsatian Smothered Worm." Dredged in seasoned flour and sautéed with onions, the worm was then lovingly baked in sour cream and drippings. Once Mrs. Forrester entered the scene, the worm possibilities were endless: spaghetti and worm balls, savoury worm pie, creamed worms on toast, Spanish worm and even worm loaf with a savoury mushroom sauce. The greatest hit was Whizbang Worm Delight: ice cream cake with whipped cream, sprinkles, jelly beans, almond slices and worms, of course.

I never orchestrated an actual DIY worm fry-up but if Alan was non-fiction and challenged me to the $50 fifteen worm bet, I would have been all in. I knew where to find the worms too. We often passed the "pickers" wearing headlamps, pulling night crawlers from the dewy soccer fields along D'Aubigny Creek. The pickers generally sold their dew worms to fisherman, not kids making gross bets in hopes of buying a minibike. Rockwell's book triggered me into thinking about the fine art of marrying flavours and ingredients.

It was the beginning of my edible education, sans worms.

I grew up with a steady but controlled feed of Scholastic books balanced with junky television. I contemplated Mrs. Forrester's earthworm recipes in the morning and then envied the gonzo kid cooks on the Canadian television game show *Just Like Mom* in the afternoon.

The CTV series was a spinoff of the winning formula behind *The Newlywed Show*. Hosted by a saccharine sweet husband and wife, the show aimed to prove how well children and their mothers knew each other. Between the two question rounds, the kids did serious battle in the kitchen baking something from the *Robin Hood Just Like Mom Cookbook*. The kids went hog wild, making gloppy pseudo chocolate chip cookie dough with wieners, Coca-Cola, marshmallows and relish. They had a full arsenal of barf-inducing ingredients that they could utilize in the mad flour-dusted rush of a sixty-second Bake-off. Then dear ol' mom had to guess which decadent cookie their lovely (evil?) little child made after it was properly baked. The kids walked away with big swag from Chuck E. Cheese, Playmobil and the sponsor, Robin Hood flour. The lucky dog grand prize winners jumped up and down with the announcement of a trip to Walt Disney World. The mothers walked away with a dull gut ache and craving for TUMS.

Condiments seemed so basic in the '80s. Heinz had every impromptu backyard BBQ taken care of. Ketchup, mustard, relish. Done. Ketchup also married well with Schneiders beef steakettes, Swanson chicken pot pies, Kraft Dinner, McCain crinkle-cut fries and Mexican hats. My dad's specialty (in addition to chronically burnt toast) was "Mexican hats." I'm not sure if his specialty is even PC anymore. At age forty-six, I finally wonder aloud, "Why didn't we call them sombreros?" For those who are unfamiliar, if you don't slit a piece of bologna before throwing it in the fry pan, it will balloon up in the centre and create an instant hat. A Mexican hat, naturally. Maybe it was my dad's attempt at bringing international flair into the kitchen? Regardless, the hat, when flipped upside down, provided the perfect vessel for at least half a cup of Heinz ketchup.

Come to think of it, my dad was also a salad designer like no other. It was always iceberg lettuce. Were any other greens available in the 1980s? Iceberg would be loosely torn and then promptly smothered in carrot coins (sometimes made with the crinkle cutter for dramatic visuals). There would be a diced tomato (cherry and grape tomatoes had yet to enter the scene), celery of questionable firmness and then – the *pièce de resistance*: TWO pieces of toast, slathered in margarine and crudely cut into makeshift croutons. My dad's salad bowls were towering with stuff tumbling off the sides into the waiting mouth of Xanadu, our optimistic canine Roomba.

Our household rotated through the reliable Kraft dressing lineup: Catalina, Thousand Island, French, Italian and Russian. We were epicurean

– or that's what Kraft led us to believe. Russian dressing is just a fancy global name for a blend of ketchup, mayo, relish and Worcestershire. There's actually nothing Russian about it – the dressing was invented in 1924 in New Hampshire. New Hampshire!

There was a desire to taste the world in a comfortable, well-sweetened way. Meatballs were consistently the dish du jour: Hawaiian! Hungarian! Swedish! World geography was covered in one sitting if there was a side salad. Water chestnuts made any dish instantly "Oriental" and any good church lady cookbook incorporated them into appetizers like rumaki. Our family was united in believing that the best use of water chestnuts was in rumaki form: wrapped in a bacon blanket, doused in the tarry tang of teriyaki sauce and broiled. Smartly, my mother omitted the traditional chicken liver filling. Not so smartly, we all suffered second-degree burns to the roofs of our mouths from these flavour grenades.

It makes sense that my spark dish would also be bacon-wrapped. I can tell you few things about our family trip to Freeport, Bahamas, back in 1995 beyond that heralded day on the seaside patio. What I do know is this: the tender shrimp wrapped in fatty bacon securing bites of sweet pineapple chunks and pliant cheese blew my emerging epicurean brain. While Russian dressing may have been a catalyst, this appetizer, chased with a virgin slushy Goombay Smash, made me hungry for more. I was becoming a gastronome, one molten bacon-wrapped thing at a time.

The '80s were a continuation of the heyday for tinned Mandarin oranges, canned tuna, Pillsbury crescent rolls and recipes that called for sherry. "Hello, Sherry, can you bring your famous Hawaiian meatballs to the potluck?" I've never tried the fortified wine and I'm okay with that. There are many Australian winemakers who probably wish they hadn't either. In 2010, sherry made in Australia was rebranded with humble apologies to the original stakeholders in Spain. If you happen to find yourself in Australia and dying for an aperitif, be sure to ask for *apera*, NOT sherry, if so inclined. (Note: None of this should be confused with the "Oh Sherrie" referenced by Steve Perry, but the lyrics could loosely apply.)

Maraschino cherries also had their time in the lambent sun and were often found in tandem with the undeniably heavenly imitation frozen whipped cream, Cool Whip. The Whip made its debut in 1966 and was still pleasing crowds like us. Cherries were used to decorate sorry-looking baked hams, Black Forest cakes, murky Coke floats and to garnish our undecided tongues when looking for something real to eat in the fridge. Learning to tie cherry stem knots with my tongue was decades from my radar and Fiona McKay, if you're reading this, you are legendary in my mind! Meaning, I still can't do this and am okay with giving up.

The skinny jars of sticky cherries the colour of clown noses seemed to be designed for pairing with the brilliant colour pinwheel of Jell-O.

Even the strange and peculiar snot green Jell-O pistachio pudding. Jell-O was the invincible and guaranteed cure-all for topsy-turvy stomachs, wisdom teeth extractions and broken jaws (my dad was living proof of this, having endured one from catching a fastball with his lower mandible). It was synonymous with Cool Whip too.

We always had Cool Whip in our chest freezer and Kiley and I believed it was complex enough as a stand-alone snack during TV commercial breaks. Sometimes the Cool Whip containers in our freezer were misleading. They often contained a window-kill cardinal or wren awaiting taxidermy, but with some effort, after finding a few birds covered in hoar frost, there was at least one container filled with genuine Cool Whip.

It was a simple, sugary time of innocence: ginger ale punches, marshmallow-based desserts (church window cookies, Rice Krispies treats, S'mores) and canned soup casseroles. Every church or music club fundraiser recipe book had a riff on an easy-peasy "Six Cup Salad." Mix one cup of sour cream, one cup of Mandarins, one cup of pineapple tidbits, one cup of coconut, one cup of chopped nuts and one cup of miniature marshmallows. Voila!

Every household had their own take on a savoury and sweet Jell-O delight. Nan Chapin owned this domain with her elegant "green fluff." I was crazy for it and can hardly believe to this day that Jell-O, sour cream and pineapple could be so pleasing in one fluffy, cloud-like serving. Despite being the same booger colour of pistachio pudding, it was the polar opposite in flavour profiles.

Green fluff, slop and fish eyes should have been the makings of a very fussy palate but our family had to be country creative. Pizza delivery was not an option in our neck of the woods and, for a few years, we were a one-car family, which meant there was no quick run into town to get more Russian dressing if one of my parents were working.

If we wanted salt and vinegar chips and only had a bag of Hostess regular, we had to aggressively douse the plain chips with whatever vinegar was on hand, red wine or malt, and eat them as fast as hyenas before they wilted with sogginess.

Caramel corn was achieved by unloading half a bottle of Crown corn syrup onto a bowl of popcorn. It was adhesive as all get out, clamping our molars together in less than two handfuls. If it wasn't adhered to the bowl, the homemade pseudo caramel corn was Super Glued to the couch or someone's unsuspecting long hair (most likely Kiley's).

Crude (and mostly unsuccessful) "popsicles" were made with grape Kool-Aid or tart Beep orange juice, ice cube trays and toothpicks. Our shitty popsicles were Xanadu's favourite as they only lasted about three licks before the toothpick snapped or dislodged and the popsicle fell to the grass for his enjoyment.

If my brother Dax and I had surreptitiously used the Lipton onion soup mix for homemade chip dip, the meatloaf my mom had intended on preparing took on a new form. It was always a win-win situation when Hamburger Helper had to step in. My mom also appreciated the occasional instant help from Chef Boyardee and we were thankful for the starch, sodium and artificial seasoning. However, our cat was less than impressed that the electric can opener was being used to open a tin of ravioli, not tuna. Such a tease.

"I'm in the kitchen!"

Our childhood kitchen was steeped in authentic 1974-ness. The irony was in the avocado fridge – everyone had one but "avocado" was merely a colour in my mind, not an actual thing. Guacamole was definitely not part of my vocabulary until 1992 or so, and only because of our accidental family trip to gay Puerto Vallarta. Fast-forward to 2021 and all ages can confidently join in a round of the "Avocados from Mexico" jingle. Eating avocado toast and posting about it is not just a thing, it's necessary. What came first, really? The avocado-coloured fridge or the avocado?

My mom made bold style choices long before *House & Garden* and *Architectural Digest* confirmed them. The avocado fridge was predictable but when my parents built our red brick ranch, my mom sketched blueprints that included an exposed brick wall and faux barn beams that ran the length of the kitchen. The beams were fabricated out of an industrial Styrofoam but looked legit. The plaster ceiling was scalloped like the top of a lemon meringue pie – save for a few missing meringue bits from wayward soccer balls and our heads, courtesy of my dad flinging us into the air to get giggles out of us. Until the giggles turned to sobs from our heads cracking off the ceiling.

The patterned linoleum floor saw a lot of abuse, including figure skates. Kiley and I were wimps about putting our skates on down at the pond behind our house. It was much more pleasurable to go pleasure skating when we were laced and ready to go as soon as we exited the house. The linoleum was etched more than an Etch A Sketch from our lazy, temperate leanings and my dad was constantly taking our skates in for sharpening. The linoleum can't be fully blamed for our dull skate blades – it was probably from hopping the rusty barbed wire fence and crossing the tracks, gravel and sloping hill of tall grasses.

Don't be fooled – my mom had her payback. She'd wash those Etch A Sketch floors with a liberal amount of Pine Oil and, unaware, each of us would charge through the main door of the garage, enter the kitchen and slide out of control for twelve feet across the wet floor before reaching the safety of the shag carpet at the finish line near our bedrooms.

Xanadu left his mark too but more often it was one of us leaving a mark because of his water bowl. The built-in cooktop stove, oven and cabinets occupied a tight space. Entering the main door, we could split left down the stairs to the basement, right to the laundry/pantry/cat litter or slip through the pocket door to the kitchen with an exit to the living room on the right.

Mud room design hadn't fully worked out its kinks yet so the shoe pile was the first potential sprained ankle territory to navigate. Then Xanadu's water dish, which was stepped in every other day. Drakkar had his automatic feeder in the same "pet station" – it was like a gumball machine for cats that required no coins. Dry kibble was made available 24/7 because who eats three square meals a day?

The greater reality was that dry kibble and Xanadu's slopped water bowl created a slip and crunch zone. It was not uncommon for one or all of us to hop around for a solid minute, daily, after stepping on either a piece of chicken-flavoured Meow Mix, one of Xanadu's spare rib bones hidden in the depths of the shag or a long-lost Lego piece.

The kitchen counters were a white and olive green-veined laminate and largely uncluttered (unless we had just come home from school or soccer practice). A stoneware crock held all the necessary implements and *Company's Coming* cookbooks were shelved on a short cabinet alongside the token avocado fridge. There was a trio of silver-lidded wood veneer containers of descending heights like Russian nesting dolls, designated for Coffee, Tea and Sugar. The wooden oak bread box (that had BREAD BOX engraved on the front in case anyone was unsure) was always stuffed with white Wonder Bread, brown for my dad and a dozen Kaiser buns from The Burford Bakery. On occasion there would be a dense glazed Chelsea loaf that would perfume the kitchen with cinnamon when it was toasted.

Each night the dish rack and accoutrements were hidden under the sink as though they were an embarrassment. We didn't have a porcelain frog for a sponge like my great-grandmother – instead we had about thirty dishcloths and by week's end, much to my mother's amazement, there were never any clean ones.

Like most kitchens designed in the '70s, we had a lazy Susan. The two-shelf cabinet grew lazier over the years from our aggressive spinning, searching for Zoodles or Alpha-gettis. We spun that thing like we were contestants on *The Price is Right*.

The true hidden surprise was a two-piece sticker of Börje Salming, the strapping Swedish Toronto Maple Leafs defenceman my mom had a crush on. Though #21 graced our mugs and glasses cupboard, my dad was not permitted to display his affection for Tina Turner in a similar fashion. My affection for pulling out the drawers below the counter and using them as stairs to access the bag of chocolate chips (or Baker's chocolate blocks in a pinch) in the uppers was also discouraged around the same time.

We had a peninsula, not an island, that split the kitchen proper from the kitchen/dining table where we traditionally ate, unless it was Friday, which meant Hawaiian pizza with stretchy double cheese from Gigi's and permission to eat downstairs in front of the TV. The kitchen table served what HGTV hosts now describe as "dual roomality." This is where everything went down: crafts, homework, wrestling matches, newspaper reading and contests to see if Kiley and I could land a pea in Dax's nostril. (Yes, we did! It was a highly celebrated moment.) A wall clock always read 3:40. For thirty-four years. Guests would either be alarmed or bewildered. "Oh my god, is that the time?"

There was a patio door at the end of the table but it was a real squeeze to access – it mostly served as a quick in and out for Xanadu, who had to do a flying leap off the cement ledge. There were no stairs off the slider but you could land safely enough with a careful big step. Followed by, "Close the screen!" We lived in the country and the flies that should have been happily ever after at my grandfather's pig barn less than half a kilometre up the road from us hovered at that patio door, waiting for entry. Which reminds me – there was always a fly swatter at the ready for those damn flies. It hung on a nail underneath Dax's framed Betty Crocker baking certificate.

The imposing hutch behind the kitchen table was where Drakkar preferred to sleep, provided we weren't too rowdy. The lower shelves housed my dad's grandmother's cute English Cottage Ware set complete with egg cups, a butter dish, teapot and biscuit holder. Upon reflection, it was displayed in a very precarious place with my mom's precious Blue Willow collection (see previous confessions about wayward soccer balls and being thrown skyward). Drakkar's coveted sleeping spot allowed him to double as a book-end for the dictionaries, *National Geographic* and Petersen field guides and the gruesome encyclopedic *Book of Health* with its colour photos of live childbirth and eye operations. This book was *not* ideal pre-dinner reading material. It was the *Book of Barf.*

Navigating questionable reading material, antique Blue Willow collections, spare rib bones and kibble was just the beginning. Enter Hammy. Dax wanted a hamster so badly he threatened a hunger strike. I think. It was a serious request, regardless. Kiley had an ink black rabbit (Bunbun or possibly Bun Bun) and Dax had Cocoa, a non-cocoa-coloured guinea pig in need of company. Hammy joined the family with his wrecking ball seamlessly. The ball was a simple, clear plastic design (about the size of a volleyball) designed to encourage free-range exercise for hamsters. It consisted of two halves that interlocked – or, more commonly, unlocked. Hammy was always on a crash course. The kitchen table and hutch hogged all the square footage, leaving

Hammy to bang around the chair legs like a pin-ball. Not so surprisingly, this led to several grand escapes when his ball would unlock and split in two. There would be an eerie silence not readily paid attention to and then, "*Hammy!* Hammy's out! His ball is in two!"

Those chair legs. Hammy's ultimate target! The chairs weighed more than one hundred pounds each, which meant we were forever dragging them and my dad was forever adding more seemingly non-stick felt bottoms to the legs. The felt pieces would end up on our socks or on Xanadu's back within days. The chairs were lethal all around, especially if you sat in them backwards. An innocent game of Monopoly turned into a crying fit when you tried to leave the table to refill the Cheezies bowl. All of us (except for my parents) will confess to having our thighs totally stuck in the back of the friggin' death trap design of the chair's rungs.

Other than that, it was a nice, normal coun-try ranch kitchen with pork hocks sticking out of a pot on the stove. Again, Kiley crying. If it wasn't the fish eyes it was the upright pig hooves (more elegantly called "pettitoes") in the pot of lima beans.

Upright pork trotters were the preferred op-tion versus when my dad was no longer upright because he'd fallen into the furnace duct. This happened time and time again because a bowl of cereal tasted even better with our feet stuck inside the furnace duct in the winter. Did we al-ways put the floor grate back? Well ... that part didn't register so well and created a dangerous sinkhole if you rounded into the kitchen from the pantry. And if you didn't step into the furnace duct, it was Xanadu's bowl and a 100 percent wet sock and pettitoes.

Hot Dog Day and (Soda) Pop Culture

There was always a case of Coca-Cola in the garage. My mom hated to have cans clogging up precious fridge real estate and we only drank the stuff on Fridays with pizza. It was dangerous to help yourself in the cloak of night as we had a chronic case of mice in the garage as well. The mice definitely kept our pop drinking under control.

On the much-heralded hot dog or pizza days at school, we were issued a can of pop for lunch; otherwise it was juice in a Thermos. Lois Isbister's mother smartly wrapped her cans of pop in a foil sheet. We did not follow suit. There was a lunchtime in grade three or so when I thought I had a Thermos full of ice. Awesome! Why hadn't my mother done this before? When I unfastened the plastic cup and screw cap from the top, I realized that my ice was actually internally shattered Thermos fragments. Piecing the crime scene together I realized that when I dropped my pumpkin orange *Dukes of Hazzard* lunch pail from waist-height when I jumped off the bus, this was the collateral damage.

Lunch pails in the '80s were such status symbols. In kindergarten, our class had grade eight monitors who volunteered to patrol our lunchtime. Curiously, if we ate our entire lunch, we were given a small prize like a seashell or marble. I still operate best under the same reward program. By grade four or so, pails were deemed not cool and were replaced by a boring but apparently cooler brown bag. "Don't throw it out either! It will still be good to use again!" My parents were into recycling before the word was coined. One-litre plastic milk bags served as free Ziplocs. We saved the blue plastic sleeves *The Brantford Expositor* was delivered in for snacks and broccoli elastics always found a new life cinching Premium Plus crackers together.

I had some great lunch pails in my day. I guess they are the purse of youth. Instead of Coach or Louis Vuitton, I proudly pranced around with Bo and Luke Duke, my coveted *Knight Rider* pail (sigh, David Hasselhoff, pre-*Baywatch*!) and epic *Star Wars* edition. Dax and Kiley leaned hard into the Cabbage Patch Kids, Strawberry Shortcake and E.T. franchises. I wonder what kind of pail I would carry now, provided I didn't work from home? Jane Goodall? Jennifer Aniston? Lake of Bays Brewing Co.? No. Definitely *This is Us*.

The biggest lunch pail thrill was the

discovery of Handi-Snacks. I'm grateful my parents pushed surreptitious recycling on us early on because these single-use plastic things are the kind of convenient stuff inconveniently bobbing around our oceans and in the guts of sea turtles and whales.

Handi-Snacks had two compartments: one housed a small stack of buttery rectangular crackers that broke and crumbled when you looked at them; the second contained a gob of processed cheese. Handily, as the Handi-Snack name suggested, a red plastic stick was provided to apply the cheese to your cracker in early charcuterie fashion. We went unnaturally crazy for these snacks despite my mother's exasperation at the price. It was much more economical to buy a box of Ritz and a jar of Cheez Whiz and send us to school with a butter knife. But that cute independent packaging! It got the better of us.

The all-time Thermos favourite was beans and wieners. Back then, no one was concerned about the implications of farty beans at lunch or the sewer whiff of unwrapping an egg salad sandwich. Lunch was fully enjoyed with disregard for others and a Thermos of beans was to be envied and savoured. My mom would boil wieners until they split and chop them into fat half-inch slices. Simmered in a can of Heinz molasses beans, it was a TripAdvisor five-star.

Better yet was the school-sanctioned hot dog day. We had to pre-order on a slip of paper that was sent home in our lunch pail. The dogs were fifty cents each and from morning recess onward, Mount Pleasant Public School smelled like one big wiener. I have no idea where they came from. Were the teachers boiling a thousand wieners behind the scenes? They just appeared, bloated and amazing, stuffed in a pillowy white bun. There were no raw white onions, sliced jalapenos, chopped green olives or sauerkraut to pile on. This was Mount Pleasant Public School, not a hot dog vendor on Yonge and Wellesley. We had a choice of ketchup, mustard and/or relish. I always ordered two. Corey Roberts and Jeff Kellam were a shoo-in three.

Pizza day was a later development in Mount Pleasant, most likely due to delivery logistics. The choice was choiceless: pepperoni and cheese. And the slices weren't slices, they were squares. Hot dog day was the bigger hit in my mind but a few years ago I learned that at some Toronto schools, kids have sushi and Booster Juice days. But not for fifty cents per.

To compensate for the lag between hot dog days my mom surprised us with hot dogs in our Thermos. That thing housed a genie in a bottle, really.

The four-hour wait time for a hot dog in a bun in a wide-mouth Thermos did not serve the hot dog well. Wet bun aside, I was grateful for my mother's ingenuity. I've never had to feed kids on a daily basis – just chimpanzees for six weeks in the Congo. There are days when I can barely feed myself, even though I work at the kitchen island, within an arm's reach of the fridge. Huge praise to my mother for her country creative hot dogs in a Thermos and also forgiveness for the time I thought she had poisoned me by slipping Dijon mustard into my standard ham sandwich.

We never knew what lunch was going to be – I imagine kids dictate their menu nowadays. Or, as I've seen on the news, students simply place their orders on the Uber Eats or DoorDash app for delivery to the front office of their school, to the dismay of principals and reception staff.

In the gilded DoorDash-less age, our school trialed an event that probably wouldn't fly today due to liability, gluten-free, peanut-free, vegan, dietary and religious concerns. On this designated day pre-gluten-free, pre-peanut-free, pre-vegan, pre-dietary and pre-religious awareness, we were privy to an all-in "lunch swap." At noon, we presented our pre-numbered brown bag surprise lunches to our teacher. We returned to our desks, giddy with anticipation and one by one picked a number out of a bowl and "won" the corresponding numbered lunch. Of course, there was always one token mother (and I say mother because, in my day, no fathers were making lunches) who forgot about the lunch swap. Great.

Winning somebody else's mom's sloppy tuna fish sandwich was an abomination. If you've had another household's version of a tuna sandwich, you will nod along knowing that these things can go sideways. Too much mayo. Not enough mayo. Hellmann's? Where's the Miracle Whip? Onions? Gross. Relish? Where are the real, diced gherkins? It's almost impossible to eat another mom's tuna salad. Hey, why isn't this bread buttered?

The luckiest lunch swaps included cold pizza or leftover Kentucky Fried Chicken. Richard Nott's mother always sent him to school with six homemade chocolate chip cookies, so winning his lunch was a really good score. A foil-wrapped Lois Coca-Cola was a bonus too. Luckily nobody was into yogurt back then – it was all pudding and leathery fruit roll-ups. Quaker Oats "granola bars" were just making an appearance cloaked in high-fructose syrups, chocolate chip and mini mallow-dotted disguise. Granola meant little to us. It was lumped in with yogurt as stuff the hippies or people on a diet ate.

When all else failed, our elementary school had a "cafeteria" that sold small bags of Hostess potato chips (plain or BBQ) and white or chocolate milk in small cartons. It wasn't a true cafeteria – more like a window in our gymnasium with a roller door. Chips were twenty-five cents and a carton of milk went for fifty cents. My dad would sometimes slip us quarters for a chocolate milk. But chocolate milk and chips? I wasn't even down with that. And who wanted white milk? Ever?

My dad. He still pours himself a tall glass of 2 percent while the rest of us clink champagne glasses at Thanksgiving or Christmas. "Anyone want a glass?" he will politely ask.

"Oh, Larry. *Gross*," my mother replies on our behalf.

Tai Chi Diets and the Swish Lady

When my dad wasn't pounding back the 2 percent (milk) it was Tai Chi. Or Thai Chai. Or some mispronounced variation of that. My mom had moved from working as a receptionist at a law firm to becoming a palliative care personal support worker. One day she came home with curious looking seeds in a Ziploc.

"They're cardamom pods." My natural reaction was to split the pale green spindle with my thumbnail to see what was inside. It was loaded with tiny black seeds, not unlike poppy seeds. A loose recipe was scrawled onto a piece of blank paper calling for steamed milk, whole cinnamon sticks, cloves, ginger, black tea and sugar.

"It's an East Indian tea."

We lived in rural Brantford, which wasn't an intentionally xenophobic area. It was simply dominated by a population of generational farmers who had migrated from Ireland or England

a hundred years ago. Sometimes the migrant tobacco workers from Jamaica who worked at the
nearby Vamos family farm would cruise down
our road on rickety 10-speeds. "Hey, Momma,"
one of the bikers called out to my mom one
blistering hot summer day. We laughed as he
dog-whistled and blew her exaggerated kisses.
Nothing was out of the ordinary except for our
bewilderment that the Jamaicans were wearing
toques and winter jackets.

In grade seven, Christine Na was my first
exposure to Chinese culture. I was so excited
to meet a Chinese person outside of Nan King
restaurant. I foolishly thought that she might
teach me how to make fortune cookies and the
neon orange dipping sauce for wontons but her
lunch resembled mine. Peanut butter and jam
sandwiches. Around the same time, my sister
was crushing on Duc Ly, a spiky-haired Vietnamese kid from West Brant she met at the public
skate night at Lion's Park Arena. We were desperate for cultural exposure and the introduction
to another exotic kitchen's menu. Though we
weren't really sure about anything ethnic beyond
egg rolls.

Finally, we were privy to Indian traditions
in our home. Long before Starbucks staked their
claim on the tall chai latte, we were grateful for
my mom's job for introducing us to the likes of
chai.

My mom's client was part of a multi-
generational Indian family and the patriarch was
ailing. Over the course of her shift, my mom

gleaned as many trade secrets as she could about Indian cooking. Chai tea was our first fragrant, global experience and instant hot chocolate was quickly pushed aside in favour of the milky, spicy elixir.

We cheated a little with the ingredients, swapping out loose black tea for bags of Tetley. Milk was simmered on the stovetop (or scalded, if I was in charge, leaving an unappealing skin on top) with cinnamon sticks, tea bags, a few cloves and pressed cardamom pods. It was so exotically perfumed and unlike anything we'd drunk before.

"Who wants Tai Chi?" my dad would ask. Though, I don't recall him actually making it – he was merely offering the idea and one of us always bit.

My dad was on a peculiar diet at that time. Tai Chi was totally part of it, in addition to pizza crusts but not pizza proper. He didn't eat apples anymore as that was the last thing he swallowed before he had a kidney stone attack. Dad also had the "yuppie flu" and that diet somehow involved dropping his daily commuter intake of a Tim Hortons raisin twist donut and double-double coffee. It was a rare moment for us to have Tim's donuts if my mom was involved. "They taste like smoke bombs. Disgusting!" She was right. It wasn't until 2006 that the Smoke-Free Ontario Act extinguished smoking in enclosed workplaces and public places like donut shops. Still, my mother's last choice for a sweet fix would be a starchy, generic Tim's donut.

Dax ruined French crullers for me long ago. "Ew. How can you stand the oil slick they leave on the roof of your mouth?" I moved on to maple dips and licking powdered jelly donuts clean of their icing sugar, as though I were a grooming cat. My great-grandmother sometimes bought the cakey powdered donuts from the in-house bakery at Calbecks. Inhale the wrong way and the generous amount of powder dusting would launch an instantaneous coughing and farting tailspin.

Everyone was dieting then, even Nan Chapin. My ten-year-old journalistic observations weren't fully fact-checked and were more of the eavesdropping variety. For example, I recorded this in my diary:

February 12, 1985: Nanny went to the hospital and will be out tomorrow. They said somethings wrong with her galdstones or she got food poisoned.

February 14, 1985: Nanny came home yesterday and is okay but she goes on this diet with no chocolate, cookies, some meats and toffee and other delicious things.

I'm guessing that "no toffee" was probably "no coffee" but I'll never know for sure. I don't think Nan put the brakes on her pot of coffee intake, especially after she pledged allegiance to International Delight French Vanilla coffee creamer. She was like watching slo-mo footage of a camel arriving to its monthly watering hole refill. *Mooorrreee cofffffeeee.* I get it now.

Nan Torti had her own diet specs as well. She was frequently witnessed eating a tin of pink salmon right from the can. She needed calcium, she told us. Which also justified her inclusion of Betty Crocker cake frosting on buttery Nilla crackers. This was the kind of diet Kiley, Dax and I could put faith in (minus the salmon). She also drank "blue milk," which I realized much later was actually skim milk (or "disgusting," as my mother indicated). Compared to fatty 2 percent, though, it is a lean and mean blue.

Nan Torti had high blood pressure, varicose veins and nerves to contend with. "My nerves!" I never understood a lot of her fretting, but she was sure to share all of her various ailments and prescriptions with us. Aunt Buffer (Nan's daughter) lived with Nan and had digestive issues to match. Buffer would eat a bag of Fritos, burp, pound her chest and announce that she needed her Gaviscon. STAT.

"Buffer's got an attack of her acid indigestion, kids," Nan Torti would inform us. One of us would jog into the kitchen to grab Buffer's Gaviscon that was kept in the fridge. Buffer was excellent at burping – an entire alphabet even, and we often wondered if her acid indigestion was cured if it would affect her burping prowess. It didn't.

Buffer served as the in-house DJ while Nan tended to our hunger needs. The vinyl would be spinning (Def Leppard, WHAM, The Pointer Sisters) and Nan would shake her hips and "knockers" (breasts) to the beat. Dax would snicker and Kiley would bounce alongside Nan while I hoped I never had knockers as big as my head.

Nan Torti kept us well-fed with sailboat sandwiches (quartered peanut butter sandwiches, placed crust-side down to appear like a boat), butter-fried hot dogs (nestled in butter-fried buns), and fish and chips wrapped in newspaper sheets from Eagle Place Fish & Chips. When it was too hot and her blood pressure was through the roof, Nan put on shorts, placed the fan on HIGH and sent us off for halibut. She wore shorts six times in ten years, too shy to show her very varicosed legs even if it was just in the company of her grandkids.

She ran a tight ship and often hollered at us to "be still!" even though she rarely was. Her fear factor came in the form of the gas stove and if we were horsing around and the pilot light went out, well, we'd all be blown to "Kingdom Come" (wherever that was).

Her kitchen was typical of wartime design: Arborite, Formica and a white basin sink with a porcelain drain board. The basin sink doubled as Nan and Buffer's bathtub. The vinyl square tile flooring resisted the abuse of the chrome diner chairs being pushed in and out (or used as ladders). That is, when the splits in the vinyl-upholstered chair seats weren't biting our asses.

The pantry had questionable shelves, all sloping with ruby red beet preserves and Mason jars of applesauce. A hatch in the floor provided access to the earthen cellar which we didn't dare enter. Even Nan didn't go down there. Instead, she stored her vegetables in the "cold cellar," which was an uninsulated room off the back of her kitchen.

Nan had a classic '50s-era Frigidaire refrigerator with a freezer that needed daily defrosting. "Everyone get out, Nan needs room. Nan needs to defrost," she'd holler in the third person. The entire contents of the freezer would be piled on the Formica table as Nan hurriedly did her thing.

If Nan wasn't chiselling away at her freezer she was on her hands and knees bleaching the floors. Every surface was sanitized to the point that we left her house smelling like Javex. Nan had no fingerprints left from her years spent as a hairdresser working with perm solution and hair dye, so she didn't mind doing the job bare-handed.

When it was cooler, and after the kitchen had a solid bleach job, we would pile in a rental car and head to Lime Ridge Mall in Hamilton, to pick up a dozen Cinnabons. The ooey-gooey rolls swirled with cinnamon, brown sugar and signature frosting were a frequent run. Nan or Buffer would lose three pounds and we became a willing part of the cloying celebration. Our teeth ached from the richness and the Cinnabons grew like a bun in the oven in our guts. But we had to cheer on the weight loss.

Everyone was watching something then. Their weight, their cholesterol. Their words.

My age five to fifteen brain didn't register calories and my 1984-1985 diary is a clear chronicle of this. In a three-day span at the end of March I recorded devouring mushroom pizza, "snacking cakes," a Coke and homemade chocolate chip cookies. The next day I was playing pinball and eating popcorn before enjoying fries from George's French Fries in addition to a bag of Hostess potato chips. On the Friday, after finishing my colouring contest entry and finding a mallard nest in our pond, I had pizza, popcorn and cake. *Then* Fudgesicles while watching TV.

I did have teeth back then – there are stacks and stacks of Kodak photos to prove it. But the sugar intake! It was mile-high! In April 1985, I learned that I needed to watch our water. The dentist informed me that I could get cavities from our water. My loose ten-year-old interpretation should have been documented like this: due to our rural property and reliance on a dug well, our drinking water was not fluoridated like the city's supply. In fact, here's a fact: Brantford became the first city in Canada to fluoridate its water in 1945.

We had a few cavities each, as to be expected – because of our well water, of course. My mom made sure our teeth were well-groomed as she faked her way through tooth-brushing as a child and teen, resulting in a very expensive adult mouth of teeth.

Still, that didn't stop me from tearing any notice from the dentist about our biannual dentist check-up into confetti thrown to the wind. We had to contend with the Swish Lady as is. Each month, the Swish Lady (probably a dental hygienist) would roll into my classroom with her boombox and fromage fest songs that we were to merrily "swish" along with. The fluoride was doled out in paper cups and we'd obediently swish and gargle the latest flavours: bubble gum, grape, watermelon. Naturally, they tasted sickly and too healthy for my liking. I didn't trust the motives behind the Swish Lady one bit. She probably didn't trust my Cinnabon and Coca-Cola intake either, so things were even.

After the gargle and unceremonious spit, we'd chew on round red tablets that would reveal the tartar on our teeth. Charming. My classmates suddenly turned rabid. It was impossible not to bare your teeth and snarl like a werewolf in response, bleeding from the gums.

Swish Lady would do her rounds, admiring our lack of tartar or *tsk-tsking* those in danger of gingivitis. It sounded terrible but surely a Coke could solve that. I'd seen the powers of Coca-Cola to remove rust from my BMX – it would definitely remove tartar if need be. Def Leppard's "Pour Some Sugar on Me" became my national anthem a few years later, in 1987.

When the Swish Lady left, our class would return to our normally scheduled programming. The lunch hour cafeteria would open up and half the class would file down to the gym for chocolate milk and BBQ chips.

I should have resembled a roly-poly bear according to my diary diet but I was as lean as a whippet. Nan Torti always asked what I weighed – as if it made sense for a ten-year-old and seventy-year-old who was two feet taller to weigh the same. Aunt Buffer and Nan Torti were large ladies, always floating between 190 and 210 pounds. They shared the same clothes and were quite confident with their figures, wearing clingy purple sweaters and animal print velour leggings unabashedly.

"Nan lost three pounds last week, how much are you weighing in at?" Nan would ask in the third person. We only knew our weight from visiting Nan Chapin, who strangely liked to weigh all the grandkids at every holiday gathering. She would diligently record our weight and height in a dedicated log book. At that innocent age, bigger numbers were coveted, even on the scale.

Nan Chapin recorded lots of things from the daily temperature to the return of the red-winged blackbirds in spring, so we didn't question her motives. I still have no idea what they could have been. She was equal parts pediatrician/ scientist/historian – who served Deep'n Delicious freezer cakes to her subjects. Nan Chapin was always trim and sturdy – she had a sweet tooth but it never revealed itself elsewhere. She was like Grandma, always outside with a few beads of sweat on her brow, stale coffee on her breath, weeds and a hoe in hand.

Nan Torti and Buffer were more likely to have Cinnabons in hand and we enjoyed their company immensely for that reason. Plus, they lived in the city, which meant water with fluoride. Sleepovers at Nan and Buffer's were risk-free. We didn't have to worry about the water giving us cavities, so we spread cake frosting on cookies with abandon. The weight of the world was off our shoulders.

Eye Candy

As country kids, procuring candy came with serious obstacles. Outside of annual restocks at Easter and Halloween, we had to stretch our inventory. A well-paced Halloween stash could last until December 1 when a milk chocolate Advent calendar would fill the countdown until Christmas. By exercising self-control (coupled with occasional thievery from siblings), the dishwater grey skies of our Novembers were made sweeter with soapy Thrills, waxy candy corn, tiny Aero and Caramilk bars and Nan Chapin's traditional pink popcorn, a very reasonable facsimile for Lucky Elephant, minus the mystery prize inside the box.

Convenience stores were wholly inconvenient to us. Our greatest opportunity to visit one was during a sleepover at Nan and Buffer's. My aunt was always keen on walking the half block to Erie Avenue to the arcade so we could play some *Dukes of Hazzard* pinball or Galaga. After we blew a sufficient number of quarters (one dollar), we'd take our grubby hands over to the self-serve candy bins at Mac's Milk. If you recall, at this point, I was relieved to learn that our well water caused cavities, not candy. And we were in the fluoridated city.

Two bucks from my dad bought a windfall of fructose. My picks never swayed from routine:
– 1 maple sugar-filled ice cream cone
– 5 Kraft Caramels (Original, not the dark ones)
– 1 strip of Fizz Wiz hard candies
– 4 Dubble Bubbles or one pack of grape Hubba Bubba if Kiley wanted to go splitzies
– 1 Big Foot
– 1 sugary spearmint leaf
– A couple of Swedish fish
– 1 pack of O-Pee-Chee hockey cards (with a bonus piece of powdery gum that was like chewing on a credit card)
– 1 Fun Dip (grape and lime as first dip picks and mostly for the addictive chalky dip Lik-a-Stix)

Dax gravitated towards the McCormicks marshmallow strawberries, gummy worms and Pop Rocks. Kiley was predictable in her leanings towards gummy bears (not to be confused with the current "edibles" in the form of innocent gummy bears), boxes of Nerds, banana marshmallows and banana runts. The shellacked runts were so hard they were like eating your own teeth. Occasionally, we'd pool our money for a pouch of Big League Chew bubble gum, packing our tiny mouths like Dax's hamster. If we had five bucks to blow, we'd go for big hitters like a bag of Bugles or pizza-flavoured Hostess chips and cans of Tahiti Treat or cream soda.

Once, I blew a whole dollar on a packet of magical Mexican jumping beans at the store. I'm sure the Canadian Border Services Agency shut down this marvel sooner than later. *"Are you bringing any food, plants, soil or animal products into Canada?"* Just a few jumping beans, no biggie!

Mexican Jumping Beans are actually seed pods from the *Sebastiania pavoniana* shrub that contain the larva of a moth native to Mexico. With heat from clammy kid hands, the "beans" or seed pods "jump" and provide cheap thrills that last as long as the flavour in a stick of Juicy Fruit gum.

Tootsie Pops and Popeye cigarettes were not popular in any of our books. Eat-More dark toffee peanut chews looked like packaged steam-rolled cat craps. And then (insert angels singing on high here) sponge toffee entered our banana seat bike and BMX radius.

In the late '80s a small market opened at the end of our road called Vine Ridge Gardens. It had one of those giant oranges that opened up into a Pac-Man shape, where employees squeezed oranges for ultra-fresh OJ. We bypassed the healthy offerings stand for the 296 ml bottles of Old Tyme Ginger Beer. Of course, Kiley and I thought we were fooling the system and buying beer underage. "We totally got away with it! They sold us beer!" We soon learned that the ginger "beer" was not beer at all and the polar opposite of my dad's staple Canada Dry ginger ale. It was like swallowing a bonfire! It was Jamaican and maybe the guys who rode past our house on 10-speeds liked the stuff and they seemed so cool.

Vine Ridge Gardens was a letdown for kids, really. The only junk food came in the form of the lava-hot ginger beer and bags of sponge toffee. Don't get me wrong, sponge toffee (or "honeycomb toffee") is essentially one hundred percent brown sugar sold in a hand-held form. You can feel your teeth melt away as you eat it. Outside of these two items, Vine Ridge Gardens was total organic this and that. Swiss chard. Field tomatoes. Peaches 'n' Cream corn. Organic. Boring.

In hindsight, all my hours devoted to breakdancing and lawn darts burned off my calorie intake like an Everest climber. I lived in the saddle of my banana seat and BMX bike. If Nan Torti kept pace and rode behind me, she wouldn't have needed to forego her Kentucky Fried Chicken skin. Which she did. Her special and exclusive custom diet involved KFC breasts – but only if the skin was pulled off. Kiley, Dax and I went into piranha mode when this happened. Nan didn't eat pizza crusts either – but my dad did. They certainly kept us on our Kangaroo-shoed toes in those days with their wacky diets.

I thought nothing of following up a Ponderosa sundae with all the available toppings (rainbow sprinkles, crushed peanuts, chocolate syrup, chocolate chips) with a milkshake at home. My mom had a penchant for Neapolitan ice cream which cramped my milkshake style. I wasn't crazy about strawberry ice cream so I had to go deep in the three-layer carton from Chapman's, avoiding the bordering strawberry that tainted the vanilla's edge.

In the hazy summer of 1985, my mom bought us reusable plastic "crazy straws" that were bent in a looping figure eight formation. Crazy straws were awesome for straight-up pop but trying to suck up a thick milkshake was enough to rupture a few neurons. The downfall of the crazy straw was the inability to fully clean the tight loops. There was nothing worse than sucking with all your might and choking back flakes or clots of dried dairy debris, stuck in the straw's bend, from long ago.

Coke floats were not a crowd pleaser in our household. Vanilla ice cream and Coke? Nope. The murky mix looked like something Xanadu would throw up in the field after eating something questionable on our walk around the pond.

However, "swamp water" was a sensation. In nearby Paris, Ontario, a donut shop gained a strong kid and teen following when word got out about their swamp water. It was a mix of all their fountain pops in one pail-sized take-away cup. Root beer, Coke, CPlus and Sprite swirled together in one potent mix left us unnaturally excited about everything except bedtime.

The swamp water was normally preceded

by a visit to Paris Fish 'n' Chips. My dad would take us pleasure skating at the Paris Arena and after practising our snowplow stops and fisticuffs in the corner inspired by Maple Leaf captain Rick Vaive, we'd refuel with a greasy load of fish and chips. If that weren't enough, we'd stop at Wendy's General Store on Grand River Street North for hockey cards and, most likely, a Crunchie chocolate bar. Coffee Crisp for Dax. Crispy Crunch for Kiley. Oh Henry! for my dad. My mom's chocolate bar choices were more sophisticated and would involve a trip to the Brantford Mall to Laura Secord's to procure French Mint bars. I can see my mom slicing just a tease from the bar. She'd ceremoniously place it on her tongue and you could watch her eyes roll back in her head like a Vegas slot machine.

The French Mint bars were the adulterated version of our preferred Cadbury Pep patties. That is, until one of us had a cough that we couldn't shake and the Vicks VapoRub ointment would appear and anything menthol received an eye-roll of a different sort.

It was a candy-coated childhood of Swedish fish and swamp water a-plenty.

Al Dente

There was obvious Alanis Morissette irony in our morning routine. We'd sit barely an arm's length from the monster console TV to take in a big gulp of cartoons with our bowls of cereal. Cross-legged on the shag, we'd watch *Simon in the Land of Chalk Drawings*, *Romper Room* and *The Toothbrush Family* to ease into the dreaded school day ahead.

For those unfamiliar with the Australian animated TV series circa 1979-1983, *The Toothbrush Family* was a multi-gen affair. Parents Tom and Tess had kids named Toby and Tina – and don't forget Gramps. Hot Rod Harry (the electric toothbrush) and Susie Sponge kinda stole the show. Regardless, the high-impact message was that we should brush our teeth round and round. The ditty was catchy and contagious. We sang along with dribbling mouths full of half-mashed Boo Berry, Franken Berry or Count

Chocula. I think I'd throw up after eating a bowl of any of those current day.

Breakfast cereals have definitely evolved and dissolved into impossibly sweet overkill on the 2022 shelves. *Introducing Tim Hortons Timbits Birthday Cake or Chocolate Glazed cereal!* Hershey's Kisses are no longer exclusively found neatly wrapped in a foil twist – you can enjoy Kisses in your cereal bowl too. Several traditional chocolate bar and cookie brands have been modified for breakfast inclusion: Reese's Puffs, Oreo-O's, Chips Ahoy! Every box, save for All Bran and the hay-like Quaker Muffets, is glazed like a donut.

The Cereal Box Club, a monthly subscription service based in Toronto, has tapped into the adult-sized kid palate reared in the '80s. They offer rare and limited-edition cereals that can be delivered to your doorstep. Our boxes were delivered by my mom's Pinto, and at her discretion. We always had three on the go, desperate for the promised prize that was included in every box. Once the prize was found, our enthusiasm for the cereal went kaput. Apple Jacks was a no-go. Frosted Flakes, Froot Loops, Lucky Charms and Cap'n Crunch were deemed acceptable by all parties. Honeycomb dislodged a few loose baby teeth so it wasn't a fan favourite – it also packed up on your molars like cement. Even if the entire *Toothbrush Family* came to the rescue, that impenetrable mortar layer of Honeycomb was often with you well into lunch.

Rice Krispies was not considered a winning option as the Krispies went to cat food mush if you lost focus on a commercial. The Krispies absorbed milk like an extraterrestrial sponge, talking in their strange and signature Krispie whisper. They really shone when mixed with melted marshmallows and butter. My mom, never shy to tinker with a recipe, would add gobs of peanut butter to the back-of-the-box recipe and melt down the giant Easter-issued milk chocolate rabbits that we gave up on. Nothing could ever be too sweet in my mom's mind.

On road trips to the States, we'd load up on Cinnamon Toast Crunch before it made its celebrated move across the border. Dax would hoard the Kellogg's Cracklin' Oat Bran which somehow became "his" cereal and hands-off to the rest of us. My parents still bring back boxes for Dax when they do an eastern seaboard run. The golden oats and fairy dusting of cinnamon and coconut are a precursor to total eating amnesia ... provided you can battle Dax and his muscle-bound frame away (then and now). On those same road trips, we'd beg and whine for the mini packs of eight assorted cereals. Raisin Bran was the throw away (Dad!) and even though it wasn't economical, those little boxes with the perforated seams and wax paper that could hold milk without a flood were a marvel. Like a North American bento box, really.

In a pinch (like, a really desperate one), Cheerios made their way to the table. Even my mom added spoons of sugar to her bowl and we followed sweet suit. Once or twice a year a bag of pink grapefruits would come home in the brown paper grocery bags from Calbecks. Like Cheerios, these were split in two and layered in sugar like a February snowfall. I can still taste the metallic tang of the special serrated silver grapefruit spoons that were put into circulation if dishes weren't done. Eating Cheerios with a grapefruit spoon is like cutting construction paper with left-handed scissors in grade three. Not fun.

Weekend breakfasts shifted from cereal to my dad's signature Mexican Hats, my mom's pancake stacks (from scratch) or soft-boiled eggs served in cute cups. We'd go on stretches of buttery DIY cinnamon toast. White toast was preferred and lovingly smeared with butter (the butter dish showcasing our careless crumbs from messy knives) and liberal dashes of cinnamon sugar. Guaranteed, one of us would be too aggressive and when the shaker left the powdered cinnamon spice container the cloud of dust would reveal more powder than toast. "Scrape it back," my dad would say and take over, shovelling the cinnamon powder back into the bottle with clenched teeth. If he was in charge of the toast production, the slice would already be well-charred. My dad was great at scraping in those days. He'd scrape the blackened toast, disguise the imperfections with more butter and then scrape back the accidental cinnamon as necessary.

I tried taking matters into my own hands by making cinnamon toast in my Holly Hobbie electric oven. Two 100-watt lightbulbs served as the heat source and it didn't take an expert to realize that I'd have to put my slices in before bed to expect any kind of crunch by morning. The bread would be well-lit but barely browned by the bulbs. At this point, I had yet to meet any Dutch friends who could have introduced me to the ultimate alternate: buttered toast with chocolate sprinkles (*hagelslag*).

Shortly after I decommissioned my Holly Hobbie oven, my dad stole what should have been my signature recipe: Egg in a Nest. I had attended a cooking workshop at Farringdon Hill Enrichment Centre in grade two and learned to make this pleasing breakfast entrée under the tutelage of a notable Brantford chef (who wasn't notable enough for me to remember their name). I demonstrated my culinary skills at home the very next morning, preparing breakfast for the family just as Laura Ingalls Wilder probably did.

Some may question the likeness of my Egg in a Nest to the American take on the English pub classic, Toad-in-a-Hole. It would take a PhD deep dive to explore what came first – the egg or the toad? The nest or the hole? Perhaps it's a mere matter of geographic designations. A classic Toad-in-a-Hole includes sausage links baked in a Yorkshire pudding-esque batter. Egg in a Nest doesn't call for bangers – just butter, bread and an egg. The secret hack is this: buttering the shit out of both sides of bread and cutting the centre out of a white bread slice using a glass as an impromptu cookie cutter.

By 1989, my dad had finally collected the

entire set of Petro Canada's Limited Edition 1988 Calgary Olympics souvenir glasses. These were *not* to be used in Egg in a Nest production. He had to buy nearly $10,000 of gasoline to acquire the set and raised his eyebrows when we became careless, sticking red licorice straws into our gas station glasses filled to the brim with Coca-Cola. Tasting notes: a piece of licorice (black or red) in a glass of Coke will turn furry and gummy in no time. Skip the straw. Just as Coke took the rust off my BMX bike frame, it also turned licorice whips into the consistency of a dead goldfish body.

Back to breakfast: the egg gets cracked square in the nest (hole) and fried up with the cookie cutter circle of bread (which is the best part and another vehicle for ketchup). You need to flip it, so patience is paramount; otherwise your nest will be a mess.

My dad kept close watch and mastered my Egg in a Nest in no time. I was okay with this because at age seven, I wasn't keen on making breakfast for the entire family. Especially when I could be sleeping or watching *The Flintstones* or simply petting Xanadu with my feet warming in the furnace duct.

I'm just thinking out loud here – what a shame that we didn't think to marry our recipes to create Egg in a Mexican Hat!

When Dax was nearly eye-level with the stovetop, he began making icing sugar-dusted crepes for the family. There was no Food Network to inspire this move – he was just a natural in the kitchen and dead curious when Kiley and I weren't. We were there to eat, not dabble, and when it came to doing the dishes, either way, we were outta there. To brush our teeth, of course. Round and round.

Our kitchen cupboards were consistent with the following smears: Kraft peanut butter (also with crumbs in it), Welch's grape jelly, Billy Bee honey (always crystallized and overlooked unless someone was willing to excavate the surface to sweeten a cup of tea). My mom made strawberry and raspberry jam that was on the same sweet Richter scale as Hershey's Kisses cereal. The occasional appearance of marmalade (for my dad's sake) was tried and abandoned for its ick factor. It was assumed to be the terrible cousin of spumoni ice cream with the bits of candied fruits and rinds (which I surmised were green and red peppers in spumoni ice cream disguise).

Kellogg's Eggo Waffles and Toaster Strudels were isolated to sleepovers at Nan Chapin's. If Grandpa was moose hunting or fishing with the guys, we took turns sleeping over with Nan. Bonus: we could pick out any junk we wanted for our stay (in addition to her favourable inventory of Chips Ahoy! cookies, Cheezies, root beer and freezer cakes. For breakfast we could have any ol' toaster treat we wanted and Pillsbury Toaster Strudels fell straight from heaven. The icing packet was applied after toasting and even with the additional application time, the cherry filling inside the strudel was like swallowing the earth's magma. I liked the creative expression that Toaster Strudels allowed. You could make a hippo out of icing, write your name, slather it on like sunscreen or just empty the packet's content on your tongue. The end result, any which way, was wonderful.

Eggo Waffles were coveted for their ability to absorb so much Aunt Jemima's syrup. Despite living so close to actual sugar bushes in Elmira and Elora, and Mennonites hand-producing 100 percent genuine maple syrup, we relied on Aunt J. The waffles weren't the best thing to feed Xanadu bites of because the adhesive syrup clung to his moustache for the rest of the day. He licked his furry lips obsessively, like I do when I realize I don't have lip balm on my person. Panic licking.

Normally we'd enjoy shortcut versions of cocoa – instant hot chocolate powder heaped into boiling water from the tea kettle. It often came with miniature marshmallows in it for a true instant experience. The marshmallows were quick to adhere to the roof of your mouth as well, and it didn't seem to matter if it was genuine hot cocoa or corner-cutting hot cocoa – we burnt the roof of our mouths all the same.

Unwrapping Christmas

"It's piping hot, don't scald your mouth," my dad insisted as he set down my cup of hot cocoa. This was premium Fry's Cocoa, stirred into hot 2 percent milk with a generous amount of sugar so our faces didn't squirm with the bitterness. It was a Christmas morning tradition – one my dad sneakily didn't participate in. Who hates hot chocolate? My dad apparently, though I didn't learn this until 2020.

Christmas morning was celebrated with Fry's and regulation-size marshmallows, the kind reserved for campfire roasting (flambéeing). It also meant the annual unveiling of the Santa mugs. They would emerge from safekeeping, wrapped in multiple sheets of *The Brantford Expositor* to prevent breakage. The mugs were pure evil due to the design flaw of Santa's hat. The end of his hat had a pompom which doubled as the handle, which was hollow. After two tentative sips, the next gulp unleashed all the hot cocoa that had channelled into Santa's pompom. Every year we forgot about the hot plume that would shoot out when least expected, like a backdraft, thus scorching the roof of our mouths, just like my dad pre-warned. Maybe that's why he wasn't a fan of the stuff. Fry's Cocoa. Fry your mouth!

The other once-a-year occurrence was the grand lighting of the fireplace. After we burnt the shit out of our mouths and sobbed, my dad would smoke us out with a fire. He'd forget to open the flue and the haze would settle just below our meringue pie ceiling. Kiley would cough like she needed an iron lung and the front door would be opened to get the air circulating again. Snow would be blowing in more efficiently than the smoke blowing out.

After worries about carbon monoxide poisoning subsided and the chirping smoke detector had its battery pack removed, everyone settled down and assumed their places. The local radio station, CKPC, would be turned up so we could listen to the carols – which was great for about ten minutes and a total bummer if we were given a new cassette tape in our stocking because we could listen to *only carols* on December 25. Dad's festive rules (still enforced to this day). Even if we had all suffered third-degree hot cocoa burns. There was zero sympathy when it came to the carols and endless *rumpapumpum* playlist.

The fire would eventually be roaring in a Norman Rockwell kind of way. Cue up David

Bowie and Bing Crosby's "Peace on Earth"/"Little Drummer Boy" mash-up.

The red velvet stocking unloading came first, personalized with our names in silver glitter to prevent fist fights and arm biting. Some of the items were both predictable and well-anticipated. Vanilla Tic Tac mints! A carton of Whoppers malted milk balls! From Woolco, there were boxes of Neilson Willowcrisp chocolates with flaky peanut butter centres (for Kiley) and Neilson Original Macaroons (for me) that resembled tiny (but delicious) chocolatey coconut turds. Dax always received a package of red pistachios. Back then, pistachios were dyed red (instead of being sold in their natural green state) to hide the stains from traditional harvesting methods. The dye was very effective and Dax would routinely have pink fingertips until the new year.

My dad would get a box of Fiddle Faddle caramel corn and Neilson Slowpokes as they were a kissing cousin to the Oh Henry! bars he loved, loaded with caramel and peanuts. He'd also get a box of the German Toffifee's which my mom steered clear of due to their superior dental-filling-removing superpowers. If the nougat and caramel didn't get to your filling first, the hazelnut hidden inside the chocolate button would. Instead, my mom was plied with a surplus of her favoured Laura Secord French Mint bars which disappeared into her top-secret chocolate vault (which I never did locate).

After our stocking reveals of underwear, invisible ink books, Freshen-up gum (the kind with the liquid burst centre), Duran Duran tapes, Rubik's cubes and the like, we'd pause for breakfast. "The trick to French Toast is frying it up in the bacon fat." My mom still abides by this guiding principle and she's never been so right. She'd slip out of the hazy living room to start the pound of bacon sizzlin' and whisk eggs laced with vanilla and cinnamon for the dunked bread.

After another dose of not-so-hot hot cocoa, surreptitious mouthfuls of macaroons and a plate of French Toast immersed in Aunt Jemima, it was game on. The entire day was sugar-laden and our garage doubled as a makeshift bakery. My mom made it all: Nanaimo bars, perfect short-bread dusted in icing sugar with pecans placed just so. There were rich coconut macaroons and melt-in-your-mouth no-bake church window cookies with coloured marshmallows rolled in co-conut. To this day, no other mother comes close. I'll be polite and praise any attempt at short-bread, but my mom nailed it. Dax (using my mother's recipe) secured second place long ago.

If my mom had a food truck, she could serve scoops of her Nanaimo custard-flavoured butter icing. The yellow layer in the Nanaimo bar was cherished. Kiley and I established the art of eating them too. The top layer of chocolate ganache could be easily nibbled off (especially if it had been in the sub-zero garage). If the bars had been inside at room temperature, we switched to licking the surface until we hit yellow. Next, the graham wafer and shredded coconut base had to be delicately chipped away at until the final heaven-sent bites of butter icing. This methodology wasn't foolproof and would sometimes result in my mother yelling from the garage: "Who's eating the top layers off the Nanaimo bars?" The base was good but, as we all know, the guts were best. My dad was impartial and ate them python-style, swallowing them whole.

Nan Chapin was known for her chocolate haystack cookies made with chow mein noodles, peanuts, peanut butter and chocolate chips. My mom's stacks were always sweeter as she didn't use the semi-sweet chips (and probably added double the chocolate chips in general), but Nan got the full haystack cred, going into mass annual production for the giant Chapin Christmas Eve dinner.

The haystacks were dangerous and divine. I discovered new-found appreciation for Xanadu's gagging fits when he managed to lodge a stick horizontally across the roof of his mouth. He'd sneeze, hack and paw at his face, drooling all the while. I'd stick my finger in and pry out the slobbery stick and he'd be off and running again. Lodging a chow mein noodle in my mouth in the same Xanadu manner was always awkward. There was always a fleeting moment of panic when trying to work it out with the power of my tongue: What if my tongue became stuck in a backwards position, trying to push the offending noodle out? Regardless, the incident didn't slow down my intake (or Xanadu's affection for stick chomping).

Nan Chapin also made classic shortbread dotted with bits of waxy green and red maraschinos. Reliably, she'd also have an endless supply of pastel chocolate mint wafers showcased in special dishes (even before dinner!). I don't remember Nan Torti baking, ever. Instead, she was an enthusiastic thrifty shopper and her pantry shelves had perennial boxes of Nilla wafers, raspberry-filled Viva Puffs and my rainy day go-to, Peek Freans Fruit Crème biscuits with their dainty raspberry/strawberry/generic red fruit centres.

Fast-forward to Christmas Day 1994, deep in the soupy jungles of Costa Rica: I fantasized about all of these cookies and sweets like long-lost lovers as I pushed around a plate of greasy canned mackerel and rice harder than my teeth.

Fortunate Cookies

"You'll get worms from eating that batter," my mom assured me. Raw or baked, her peanut butter chocolate chip cookie batter duped us into agreeing to do anything. "Yes, I'll polish all the louvre closet doors with orange oil! I'll vacuum the shag!" It was a smart negotiating ploy on her part – and she was right about the worms.

In 1995, after my three months in the Costa Rican jungle, a specialist at the Tropical Disease Clinic at McMaster University in Hamilton identified three different types of parasitic worms in my gut. My mom said we'd get worms from eating raw potatoes and half-cooked spaghetti noodles too, so this explained everything. My parasites had nothing to do with the steamy jungle and drinking tainted river water in Alto Cuen. It was that darn cookie batter from 1984!

My mom never flattened her cookies with a fork. Instead, they were rich golf ball-sized delights that could be swallowed in one go, if need be (i.e., running for the school bus). They were so studded with chocolate chips that the peanut butter batter could barely glue them together. Her banana chocolate chip muffins were made by employing the same ratio. A few bites in, we all looked like we'd been eating mud, chocolate streaking our tiny teeth as we enjoyed bananas in the best form possible.

The cupboard in the kitchen island housed the cookie and chip cartel. Oreos were a mainstay and Kiley and I ate them like a three-course meal, layer by layer. The Oreos we took to school for recess were never fully enjoyed as unabashedly licking the icing off in public was frowned upon, even by our schoolmates who wanted to do the same.

All sandwich-style cookies were deconstructed, mostly to prolong the experience. Christie Fudgee-O's (made with real cocoa) were subbed in if Oreos weren't on sale. Then, Oreo only had two versions: Double Stuf and the mint cream-filled Grasshopper which was blacklisted by all of us. Who wanted to eat a cookie and a mint at the same time?

In 2019, there were seventeen different Oreo flavours including Marshmallow Peeps, Red Velvet, Birthday Cake, Fudge Dipped Coconut and Cinnamon Bun Crème. The team at *Food & Wine* nibbled and ranked them in a nod to National Oreo Day (March 6, hello!). Oreo Original won – that's just the way the cookie crumbled.

My kid brain never imagined the likes of Birthday Cake-flavoured Oreos or, better yet, deep-fried Oreos. In 2012, my sister joined me on a press trip to the Edmonton Folk Music Festival and nearly passed out from the flavour rocket that was discovered in golden-battered deep-fried friggin' Oreos. The entrepreneurial vendor had a snaking lineup for good reason. People were leaving Blue Rodeo's performance for these cookies, that's how serious the situation was.

Funny, I don't remember ever seeing my mom eat an Oreo or Fudgee-O. Bi-annually, a bag of Christie's Pirate Oatmeal Peanut Butter cookies appeared and grew stale. Dad's Oatmeal were suitably only enjoyed by my dad in addition to his "baby cookies" (Mr. Christie's Arrowroot Biscuits). Oatmeal! Baby cookies! So healthy! We were not going to be tricked! My dad was also in charge of eating the "white" cookies in the Girl Guide boxes. *"Do not* eat the chocolate ones," my mother coached him.

Even when Kiley was a Brownie, she sold Girl Guide cookies. I think it was part of the grooming process. They were two dollars a box then. Thirty-five years later they are five bucks a pop and you can buy them at the grocery store alongside Oreos. What happened to door-to-door marketing? The cookies are now kosher and produced by Dare Canada in two annual campaigns. The classic chocolate and vanilla sandwich cookies are available in spring while the "Chocolatey Mints" are exclusive to fall.

Peek Freans' Assorted Cookies were exclusive to Nan Torti's and available year-round. My aunt Buffer and I would challenge each other to arm wrestling battles over the Fruit Crèmes, despite her age, size and weight, which should have disqualified one of us. The true prize was in the bottom tier of the four assorted choices: the rectangular chocolate sandwich cookie. It took a child's hand to nimbly slip into the space between the accordion paper and the bag to access the bottom layer and fish out the lowest cookie.

Nan Torti's pantry was also reliable for a stash of Bargain Harold's Voortman Strawberry Wafers and soft Raspberry Turnover cookies with the gob of jam in the middle. The wafers were like eating pink-coloured paper, mostly, but the layers of strawberry icing redeemed the questionable nature of the cookie. Voortman also made Windmill cookies, a take on the gingery Dutch *speculaas* with shaved almonds that were thinner than an eyelash. At Christmas we could count on Voortman's Festive Cookies in the shape of a wreath. They were dredged in green sugar crystals and coloured round sprinkles or "nonpareils" in baker-speak. "You can't eat those in the car!" my dad would cringe. Just looking at the Festive Cookies made the sprinkles fall like candy dandruff.

A safer in-car cookie was a box of McDonaldland crunchy animal cracker-like likenesses of Ronald McDonald, Birdie, Grimace, Hamburglar and Captain Crook. The cookies that were introduced the same year as me (1974) were sadly discontinued in favour of "gourmet" chewy, bakery-style cookies in the '90s.

We were fortunate to grow up exposed to so many cookie brands courtesy of our doting grandmothers. Still, we were versatile, not spoiled. We were schooled in the benefits of anticipation and patience. In a country pinch, we'd fashion our own sandwich cookies out of Honey Maid graham crackers with over-the-top smears of Kraft smooth peanut butter.

Add a Styrofoam cup of muddy hot chocolate from the hockey arena's vending machine and I wanted for nothing. Except for maybe a surprise production of my mom's pillowy pigs in a blanket after a solid day of practising my crossovers and snowplow stops behind the blue line.

Pigs in a Blanket

I could always detect the pigs in a blanket at fifty paces. The buttery dough and salty wiener scent of childhood umami rode on the air like a kite and filtered under the garage door as the most beautiful "welcome home." After a grass-stained soccer practice or shivery afternoon in the arena bleachers watching my dad play hockey, sniffing pigs in a blanket erased the day. My mom made the dough from scratch, without an assist from the sticky, apocalyptic-surviving whack-and-twist Pillsbury Crescent Roll.

The blanketed pigs were better received than the pig hocks hanging out of the stock pot. French's mustard was the only condiment necessary and on those treasured nights, despite being zero percent religious, we thanked God for having pig farmers in our bloodlines. The word "vegetarian" meant nothing to anyone, yet. At least not in our pork-friendly household. Vegan and vegetarian were as foreign as Birthday Cake Oreos, Crystal Pepsi (circa 1992), Senegal and Taylor Swift.

Allegedly, pigs in a blanket are a borrowed concept from the Belgians. The traditional "dish" is connected to the city of Namur. "*Avisance*" is sausage wrapped in bread dough – although tradition has shifted in Belgium too, in favour of the ease of puff pastry.

Wieners were probably the beginning of the food fusion movement. On a stick, voila! Corn dog. Chopped into one-inch dimes, voila! Heinz beans and wieners! Tossed in Kraft Dinner! On a longer stick, over the fire – oh, whoops. Charcoal. Embers. Nowadays, kids are privy to mommy blogger camping trends like "spider dogs." Cutting a regular hot dog in quarters on each end (leave one inch in the middle intact) will create eight "legs." Splay them over a fire and the cut ends will curl up like a Toni home perm.

We didn't know spider dogs but I'm sure they would have been something we had a tantrum over. What we did have was a version of "cheese dreams." White Wonder Bread buns, split, smeared with Cheez Whiz and latticed with raw bacon. Thrown under the broiler the bacon would sizzle, crisp and the cheese would turn into a fondue glue. All of this was eaten lava hot, to finish off a just-healed roof of my mouth. The cheese would bubble into a black plastic film at the edges (delicious!). If someone wasn't looking, they lost their bacon strip quite quickly. We called them cheese buns and the recipe never veered. If there was no bacon, there were no cheese buns. You could *not* sub in wieners.

Some of my classmates spoke of "Cheese Dreams" made with Kraft Singles. Head-to-head, the Singles paled in flavour to the rich, savoury body of Cheez Whiz. For us, Cheez Whiz had two roles: cheese buns and celery sticks. We weren't forced into eating celery that often, but when it did present itself, it was totally acceptable to fill its groove with Cheez Whiz. It became tongue and groove as we recycled the celery for free cheese refills. Current day, the only point I see in celery is as a straw to swirl horseradish-flecked Caesars. You only have to half-swallow a celery string once to forever remember the feeling of something like a cat's whisker halfway down your esophagus and sticking halfway out of the back of your throat. I fully understood our cat's full body purge efforts into expelling a furball.

If my dad was in charge, Kraft Singles were put to good use in the form of his famous "cheese grilled." Never grilled cheese. My mom's version was oozing full of Cracker Barrel cheddar that stretched an arm's length before the face slap when it reached its elastic end. Her grilled cheese sandwiches were so buttery you had to make a barricade with your hand when carrying them downstairs on a plate. One misstep and the slippery, buttery sucker would slide off and ride down the stairs, usually in a trail of ketchup blood.

My dad's cheese grilled differed as it was toasted. Or blackened, to be truthful. After the signature char scraping, margarine would be scraped across the charred surface, topped with a Kraft Single, pressed with his own hand panini and cut in half. We appreciated both takes of the grilled cheese and cheese grilled because, well, ketchup. Dad was just as practical in his drink offerings. "Do you want a glass of milk or a Wink with that?" By wink, I don't mean the affectionate eye expression – I'm referring to the grapefruit-flavoured soda that my parents mixed with gin. At age eight, after my first wink-inducing Wink, I decided to wait until nineteen to drink Wink as it was designed. With gin.

At this point, my mother is probably yelling at the pages of this book. What about my beef stew with dumplings? My oven rotisserie chicken? Beef chili? Chicken cordon blue? Caesar salad? Spaghetti and real meatballs!

One would think the Torti kid diet was composed of only potato chips, wieners, frosted cereal, fake cheese and cookies. That's nostalgia for you. Ask me about my four months in Africa and I won't even think of mentioning the dust that penetrates everything from your nostrils to your socks. The tsetse flies that land inside your ears and try to land on your eye iris. Getting squashed in the back seat of a mutatu taxi with a bag of charcoal, a wet and punky 200-pound Nile perch, a car battery, a few live chickens, nineteen Ugandans and a hundred pounds of bananas. Instead, I'll tell you about all the good stuff.

Despite what my age ten diary chronicled we were seemingly spoiled by a lot of junk, but we did eat a lot of good-for-us stuff too. Like that thick beef stew with carrots and potatoes that gave way to the broth. Giant seasoned dumplings that absorbed the unctuous gravy-like base into bite-sized tickets to satisfaction. Yes, we had our share of soggy McCain fries and High Liner fish sticks, but six out of seven days of the week were homemade, from-scratch dinners. Come to think of it, those fries and sticks were usually pushed on us by teen babysitters or Nan Torti, who was only comfortable at her gas stove-top (but could work the oven dial).

My mom's spaghetti sauce would beat the pants (and flour-dusted apron) off any Nonna (or Nan). Beefy, garlicky and chunky with stewed plum tomatoes, we'd dip half-boiled spaghetti noodles into the simmering, splattering sauce as teasers (despite the "you'll get worms" warning). There was always oven-baked garlic bread too, saturated in butter and garlic salt, perfuming the entire house with warm, loafy goodness. If Calbecks didn't have any loaves, the Wonder Bread hamburger buns would be subbed in.

I polled my family in the early stages of writing this book and without prompting or swaying from each other, my mom's spaghetti sauce found a place on four out of five Torti lists. I asked Kiley and Dax to list their three favourite things that Mom made during the '80s. I asked my parents too in case I had missed some potholes that they could fill on my memory lane.

Confirming the unanimous winner, my mom also cast a vote for her own spaghetti sauce (and chocolate macaroons, rightfully so). Everything she made was amazing hot or cold or half-cooked, whether it was the batter or the dregs.

Kiley continues to make my mom's spaghetti sauce verbatim, and that's saying a lot. She's not one to hang around in the kitchen (only to eat) as her husband Mark demonstrated his prowess with portobello risottos and seared scallops long ago.

My dad voted spaghetti without blinking and, curiously, fried bologna. Mexican Hats (a.k.a. fried bologna) was essentially his signature dish. He also voted for Eggs in a Nest (*mine!*). Dax glazed over with the savoury recall of my mom's oven-baked back bacon. He ranked it narrowly above her broccoli casserole. What kid (or adult) picks broccoli casserole as their favourite thing Mom made? But I should explain – this casserole had more cheese than mac 'n' cheese. It was laden with buttery croutons that were baked into a crispy crust. The broccoli barely registered. I do recall her saying, "Now you can't just take the crust!"

Kiley and I aligned in votes for Mom's cabbage rolls. She refuses to make them now for big gatherings and not for labour intensive reasons. "They look like tobacco worms!" She's right, but those worms were her grandmother's (my great-grandmother's) recipe and made with a sweet tomato sauce laced with three tablespoons of honey and brown sugar that no one can match. Same with her turkey and roast beef gravy. It was rare that we were at Nan Chapin's for dinner (outside of Christmas Eve and a sleepover), but my mom really should have shared her recipe with Nan. I'm glad the recipe swapping didn't go in the opposite direction.

The gravy my Nan made was off-colour and bitter. It wasn't fatty. It looked like soy sauce. My mom's gravy was as golden as a July suntan, with flecks of grease and pepper, thick with cornstarch – the gravy was way more important than the potatoes and I understood why Xanadu loved his Gravy Train dog food so much. I'd eat his kibble with this gravy. Her turkey gravy was nearly drinkable and really ruined us for Swiss Chalet and their supposedly "special sauce."

I should note that Nan Chapin redeemed herself with her classic asparagus on toast, served with a very simple "white sauce." If an afternoon of UNO and Old Maid got out of hand she'd eventually ask if we wanted something to eat. *Yes!* Wild asparagus sprouted up and down the train tracks behind our house and grew in a healthy, established rows in her garden by the koi pond.

"Go grab some asparagus!" We'd run out to the row and snap off a mitt-full of spears as she did a quick stir of melted butter, flour to thicken and generous grinds of pepper. It quickly congealed so you had to eat it lightning quick. "Put the bread down!" The toast would jump out of the toaster and be smeared with more butter. The asparagus would be boiled to death (as every veggie was back then) and laid limp across the toast. There would be so much white sauce that the asparagus would be an afterthought. Just like the decade.

As the neon lights of the '80s flickered and buzzed out with the fireworks ushering in 1990, many things remained. Acid-wash jeans, Madonna and crimping irons. The pigs in a blanket, cheese grilled and grilled cheese afternoons were a mainstay. However, we were entering the Age of Aquarius (or something like that) – Old El Paso tacos! Nachos! Bagels! Nutella! The Torti household was becoming très international, just like Madonna's "La Isla Bonita."

My formative years were just beginning.

The 1990s

Chips and Dips

"Do you want Smokey Bacon or plain with chip dip?"

"Plain with dip!"

In our kitchen, French onion chip dip came and went as fast as Halley's Comet in '86. We would extend the life of chip bag crumbs, submerging the stale chip shards into the dip until we were forced to use our index fingers as the dippers, long after the chips were gone.

"Ginger ale or Pepsi?"

My dad's peculiar diet transitioned from Coke to Pepsi (for unknown reasons), but mostly Canada Dry ginger ale.

"Pepsi!" I'd whisper-yell to Kiley as she stealthily crossed the threshold from the kitchen to the main door. My parents built a primary bedroom and bath addition to our ranch that put them in a far (but not far enough) L-shaped wing off the back of the house. Stealing pop from the

garage was still a covert mission with the ever-present threat of startling Xanadu whereby he
would launch into a barking fit. (Which I could
usually hush with a handful of chips.)

Pop and chips in tow, we'd head back to
Kiley's bedroom and sit cross-legged on her bed
with her mauve boombox on low. We'd listen to
Tiffany's debut solo album on repeat, hovering
over the rewind button with salty fingers after "I
Think We're Alone Now."

Upon entering grade nine at Brantford
Collegiate Institute, I became one of Kiley's most
fascinating people. Overnight, Kiley became
Barbara Walters – interviewing me, the Most
Fascinating Person of 1990. I had the inside chip
and dip scoop on high school and graduated to
Kiley's BFF for the intel I had access to.

We'd talk past midnight about how cute
Matt Macklin was, the price of cafeteria fries,
volleyball try-outs and how it was *just* like
Degrassi High. Kiley was two years younger
than me and the anticipation of joining the
Girls Athletic Society and flirting with cute
quarterbacks was killing her.

I'm not sure where Dax was when we
underwent a day-in-the-life-of-high-school dis-
section. Probably studying. This would explain
his future double degree in biotoxicology and
microbiology, PhD and current job title: Program Manager, Princess Margaret Cancer Centre
– OICR Translational Genomics Laboratory at
Ontario Institute for Cancer Research. Really. Do
you want chips and dip with that?

Dax was already light years ahead of Kiley and me in a few departments like biceps, Madonna lyrics (and associated dance moves) and baking. Most teens graduated from high school with basic microwave meal confidence (we had yet to procure one). Dax was twelve and making his own braided egg loaves, marbled cheesecake brownies and stuffed pizza breads. Kiley had attended the same 4-H Bread Baking classes as Dax but somehow managed to not retain or repeat anything from the course.

Grade eight home ec class had crudely equipped me for the real world. Yes, I had fashioned my own margarine-coloured apron during sewing class (poorly) but the only recipe I had in my wheelhouse was pizza soup. It was never a great hybrid but it was an easy chop and simmer. Pepperoni, peppers, onions and a carton of broth? Bouillon cube? Shredded cheese? Dax probably knows.

Because I was so responsible by grade nine, we weren't traipsing over to Grandma's after school for babysitting and a feed of fried smelts. Instead, my parents were confident that we could be latchkey kids for the hour or so before one of them returned home. Par-tay! The volume on our record player would be turned to BLAST level as we danced around the evil wheat sheaf table and up and over the sunset orange couch to Doctor and the Medics "Spirit in the Sky." We'd slow things down for Sinead O'Connor's "Nothing Compares to U," singing until we were hoarse. After a Pepsi break, we'd break into some serious

Madonna vogueing, interpretive dance to Wilson Phillips' "Hold On" before the dramatic sing-along to "More Than Words" by Extreme.

Dax would prep a banana split feed for himself, emptying most of the Chapmans ice cream into a mixing bowl with banana dimes, endless Hershey's Chipits and handfuls of Spanish salted peanuts. Then a drizzle of Brown Cow chocolate syrup for good measure.

Kiley and I made our own healthy snack out of Garfield cheese-bombed nacho chips. We'd shred cheese or glop on Cheez Whiz, scatter a pile of chopped green olives and bake them in the oven. Five nights a week.

Even though I was the oldest, I was never tasked with prepping dinner – unless it was putting a pot of something on the stovetop on simmer or pre-heating the oven. I doubt I was very responsible even with those simple tasks. My one attempt at making Kraft Dinner ended up as a soup. "Oh, drain the water." Duh.

Dax was the one who pointed out my error from the living room, his nose in an encyclopedia of some sort. However, if you choose to not follow the recipes and don't drain the water but still add the cheese powder and butter, you can make a rather pleasing soup. I was ahead of the ramen noodle game. Why couldn't KD be treated the same way?

At some point in grade nine my dad started bringing home hand-rolled, honeyed bagels from Montreal via his workplace, Hussmann's. A sales rep he chummed with at the food retail merchandising and refrigeration company made frequent runs to a Toronto client who was a bakery owner. My dad would buy a dozen bagels for five bucks in an early CSA (Community Supported Agriculture) box kind of operation.

We were all over the nouveau cuisine. Montreal! Or Montreal-*style*? Now I question the origin. Either way, the bagels went like IHOP hotcakes and landed on our kitchen peninsula with five-pound tubs of margarine mysteriously procured from the Valade family on Pleasant Ridge Road.

While we were slow to the microwave game, we had a Snakmaster – or the reasonable facsimile of it. It was a white Swan brand toasted sandwich maker that gave us kids such independence, elevating afterschool snacks to a new, unprecedented snack level. The perfect crust crunch and hidden envelope of cheese created a hand-held pocket of ooey-gooey divinity that made us feel so sorry for Laura Ingalls being born into the wrong time and prairie place.

Nan Chapin already had a microwave. She also had a bidet, satellite TV and a jacuzzi tub. It was a sharp contrast to Nan Torti's wartime house – she didn't have a tub at all, let alone a jacuzzi one. Nan Chapin was always on the cusp of the hot trends, which was strange for a pig farmer's wife. When the microwave was installed above her oven, we screamed up the road on our Turtle-waxed bikes. "Watch this. All you have to do is put a piece of bread in and in one minute you have toast." The microwave had a dial timer control knob that tracked the minute but it didn't stop us from watching the minute hand on her singing bird clock above the unit. We watched the birds and the bread with split eyes: purple martin, tick, Eastern screech owl, Northern cardinal, tick, white-breasted nuthatch, tick, tick, bald eagle! Ding!

She was dead right. I think a slice of bread would catch on fire after a minute in today's high-efficiency microwaves, but back then it took a while for the radon to rumble to life. We were in a trance. We stared at the magic occurring inside the microwave oven like wide-eyed children before us watching Neil Armstrong land on the moon. Nobody forgets their first microwave experience.

Our kitchen appliances were slim but adequate. The almighty sandwich maker ruled supreme and shared a shelf with the hot air popcorn maker. The tiny butter melter that served as both a kernel measuring cup and plastic guard against the searing projectile popcorn was deemed unreasonable by my mother. "Get a saucepan out – you need way more butter than that chintzy thing will allow!"

We had an Oster blender that we never rinsed after making milkshakes. There were constant empty threats: "I won't buy ice cream again if you guys won't rinse this thing after you use it." Ice cream was always available, despite our failure to rinse.

The hand-held blender matched the avocado-green fridge and should have come equipped with enough beaters as offspring. The hair-pulling over licking the beaters was always intense and usually ended with Dax doing a big territorial cough over everything. He was usually the one doing the blending, so rightly so.

My first kitchen appliance (after my Holly Hobbie oven) was a Snoopy Sno-Cone Machine, which was nothing like the commercials promised. Ice cubes were inserted into the igloo's chimney and jammed down into the sno-cone grater by a hand-held "ice pusher." A miniature red plastic shovel was provided to remove the endless slushy from the crude "blender." Day-Glo syrups and disposable paper cones were included but were depleted after a single use. With all my might the ice pusher wasn't great at pushing. The plastic crank at the back to churn the blender usually fell off or, more often, the entire igloo would topple over from aggressive grinding. Xanadu would appear in a heartbeat. "Cleanup in aisle five!" We'd try to salvage the precious ice cubes that were still intact in lieu of having to wait an entire day for another batch to freeze.

What was supposed to be a savvy solution to country living (and absence of convenience store slushies) was a disappointment. I can still taste the wayward dog hairs and carpet fibres that would end up in our cups from the retrieved roll-away ice cubes.

Millennials, if you are reading this and are perplexed, these basic kitchen implements were in circulation *loooong* before the likes of the blood red KitchenAid stand mixer with gourmet pasta press, pasta roller, 5-blade spiralizer, all-metal grain mill and sifter + scale attachments. We weren't privy to a travel-friendly BlendJet for 40-second custom smoothies and protein shakes. There was no Ninja®Pro Plus Blender DUO, no SodaStream Genesis sparkling water makers. There was no Instant Pot (unless you were friends with that guy who slept in the back of art class). Or air fryer (not to be confused with the hair fryer: the crimping iron).

Hell, Martha Stewart's first cookbook, *Entertaining*, had only been published in 1982. It wasn't until the end of 1990 that our darling lifestyle expert launched *Living*, the iconic magazine and universal housefrau saviour. Her weekly half-hour syndicated show had yet to air – that followed two years later in 1992. The same year I was introduced to Vietnamese soursop shakes at Quan 99.

My mom was revolutionizing the Torti household on pace with Martha but with *The Best of Bridge Club* cookbooks, *Chatelaine* magazine and *Wok with Yan* as fallbacks. The way we entertained (Snoopy Sno-Cone, anyone?) was changing with imported bagels and microwave toast. We were growing up. Who knew that Martha would grow up to co-host a reality TV show with Snoop Dogg nearly twenty-five years later? The parallels in our lives – it's uncanny.

Geography Class

The pedestrian-friendliness of my city high school introduced two beautiful things into my life: Rosa's Pizza and Quan 99. My cross-country running team archenemy, Stacey Hill, became a double nemesis in a month-long pizza-eating competition. She was fleet-footed and an entire foot shorter than me but could pack away a pizza slice like no other. I can't remember what the grand prize of our competition was – or if we even had one. Much like Alan and Billy's fried worm bet, Stacey and I were engaged in a head-to-head pizza battle. It was win-win really. I usually ate the lunch my mom made on the forty-minute bus ride into school (the Oreos at least) and was ready for a slice by high noon. Rosa's was one block from Brantford Collegiate Institute (BCI) and a magnet for students. Lineups would snake out the door for the $2.25 pepperoni slice and pop special. Those in the know knew to sip the pooled grease from the individual curled pepperoni cups and then fold the triangle in half, using the paper plate as a precautionary oil shield. I ruined a few T-shirts thanks to the rain of pizza grease from a drippy Rosa's slice.

My dad was always slipping me money for incidentals, which largely fuelled my pizza fund. Good thing I was running competitively and chasing Stacey Hill to the finish lines every race. After thirty days of competition pizza eating in a row (save for weekends for obvious reasons), I resumed normal programming for awhile until I weaseled my way into the home of a "walker."

We were "bus students" in elementary school too. Even though we lived five kilometres from Mount Pleasant Public, the bus ride was over an hour. We were the first ones on and the last ones off. This was a big deal as we set the pace of the driver in the morning. There was no way in hell we were going to stand at the end of our driveway and wait for the bus, regardless of the season. Oh no, the driver could wait for us. Only Mr. McIntyre had patience for our tardy ways. The new driver, Sue, barrelled past our house (picking up speed) like a Dakar Rally competitor, smirking as she ignored our hollered pleas and waving arms to stop.

Mr. McIntyre enjoyed a chuckle watching us tumbling and screaming across the front lawn, lunch pails clacking, poster projects unfurling, nearly missing the bus most days. We always envied the "walkers" who didn't have to live according to bus schedules and could walk to school on their own terms. Walkers were privy to walking home for lunch too – hot lunches of Zoodles and Campbell's tomato soup with grilled cheese sandwiches to dunk. I was envious as we were confined to our desks until everyone finished their lunch, whereby we were released into the wilds of the outdoors for a few rounds of square ball, murder ball or Double Dutch chanting. Our friendships were segregated: bus students vs. walkers. Stone-cold tuna sandwich vs. piping hot Chef Boyardee raviolis.

Until high school, that is. At BCI, I became fast friends with Liz Hart, BCI's basketball superstar. We were in almost all of the same classes: English, Phys-ed, French and History. Liz shared half of her classes with Martha Shrubsole and when we realized that we all had the same lunch period, Liz casually invited us to her house. I was friends with a walker! Finally! Liz lived a few houses off historic Dufferin Avenue in an ornate brick century home with a manicured and pedicured front lawn. She had a scrappy schnauzer named Shakespeare who loved to rip around in tight circles on the grass, happy to see Liz and new petting guests. Liz's mom was a doppelgänger for Patti LuPone, who played the matriarch, Libby, in the TV drama *Life Goes On*. Libby, as I liked to refer to her, confirmed my suspicions of the walker's routine. Hot Zoodles and simmering Campbell's soup. It was as I had imagined!

Martha was also a bus student, so we brought brown bag lunches with us and camped out in the living room picnic-style while Liz had her ready-the-minute-we-walked-in-the-door hot lunch. We had enough time to watch *Leave it to Beaver* and *The Little Rascals*. I knew the TV programs from sleepovers at Nan Torti's because she had cable but they were shows that I never watched at home. Kiley and I were a force when it came to dominating the console TV whenever *Roseanne, Growing Pains* or *Who's the Boss?* was on. Black and white television was not our thing but to be connected to a walker and to watch TV during the school week, at lunch, was a privilege.

My other privilege came later, when I discovered the distinct advantages of skipping a dull class in favour of a Vietnamese lunch. Quan 99 was always empty with both a TV (on mute) and shrine aglow. Sometimes the owner's kids would be there, colouring or crying at the table in the back.

I'd take a seat and order anything I didn't recognize (again, courtesy of my dad's allowance). Soursop shake? Sure! I had no idea that it was a prickly green fruit that tasted like a pineapple. The next visit I opted for the durian shake. Years later I learned that the fruit smells so obnoxious that it's banned from Singapore Rapid Mass Transit. As a shake it was divine, but food writer Richard Sterling accurately stripped it down to this: "its odor is best described as … turpentine and onions, garnished with a gym sock. It can be smelled from yards away." In a

Smithsonian Magazine article, Anthony Bourdain (who I didn't know at the time) commented that the durian was "indescribable, something you will either love or despise ... Your breath will smell as if you'd been French-kissing your dead grandmother."

Durian shakes became my go-to, gym sock and all.

At Quan 99 I felt very fancy, removed, independent and all-knowing, no doubt. I tried wok snow peas with silky tofu and ginger, slippery-sauced duck wings and deep-fried spring rolls with glass noodles, shredded carrot, taro and cabbage gift-wrapped in perfect pastry. I skipped French class for a serious lesson in Vietnamese cuisine – sliced, tart green mango slivers with crushed cashews, fiery chili flakes, torn cilantro and a zip of lime juice. I worked my way through the menu as though it were curriculum: crispy shrimp rolls served with thick peanut sauce, soups rich with coconut milk, galangal and lemongrass. Bamboo shoots in stir fries with fishy oyster sauce, long beans and udon noodles.

In less than a dozen sittings I had introduced myself to another planet, and I wasn't coming back. Plus, I found I could order a beer and the owner didn't flinch.

My mom has always enjoyed a late afternoon beer. My dad, never. Not late afternoon, late night – never. My sister sides with my dad to this day. Both of them will make a face like they've sucked on a lemon if a glass of red wine or a beer is offered.

Labatt's Blue was always the garage staple and when I turned sixteen, my mom would offer me a short pour of her beer. I soon found taller pours by hanging out with a group of artsy guys in grade eleven with older brothers and connections. We drank Formosa Springs and Upper Canada Lager in a responsible way (really) and Labatt's Blue paled in pale ale comparison. I suggested that my mom try a new brand, like Formosa perhaps and she was game. My dad wasn't impressed as the new brand cost a few bucks more than the Labatt's.

Derek Butler and I were in Mr. Hughes' art class together and Derek was intimidatingly talented. He would go on to enroll in Sheraton's animation program but decided to work the beat as a cop in Brantford. Still, the guy could draw anything from a car engine to any member of the Simpsons family with his left hand to a lifelike Arctic wolf or werewolf for that matter.

I was fascinated by Derek's fascination with the early twentieth century artist Tom Thomson – Derek drove three hours to Owen Sound, on his own, to visit Thomson's grave. He was crazy about American survivalist Tom Brown Jr. and his New Jersey-based Tracker School. Derek was preparing to take the course that taught attendees how to survive with just a knife in the woods, based on the teachings of Stalking Wolf, the Apache elder who taught Brown everything he abided by. If he wasn't drawing or extolling the healing properties of local honey, Derek was dog-earing *Tom Brown's Field Guide to Wilderness Survival*.

As part of his training Derek stripped away the stuff that wouldn't be available in the woods: Upper Canada beer, coffee, sugar. He became a lean machine: his Levi's jeans hung on his survival-ready frame by a leather belt that saw weekly hole punches.

Curiously, Derek's BFF, Paul, was on his own mission. Paul was locked into Dr. Robert Haas *Eat to Win: The Sport's Nutrition Bible*. Martina Navratilova was a big ambassador and soon Paul (not a tennis player) adopted Haas's diet as well. He was eating to win and drank nothing but black coffee and water and ate boiled potatoes by the bushel. Paul was already a string bean – he could have been the startling body double for bone rack Christian Bale in *The Machinist*.

I found greater kinship with Jeremy LeMarre as we shared a mutual affection for the Snakmaster. We smoked a bit of weed, glugged Pabst Blue Ribbons and inhaled midnight Snakmaster sandwiches while Derek and Paul morphed into pure muscle. Eating to win didn't look that appealing and I had no immediate plans to walk into the woods with just a knife. (Author's note: However, in 1995, Tom Brown Jr. and Stalking Wolf would have been a reassuring voice in my head when I became very lost in the Costa Rican jungle for a harrowing hour.)

I had knotted together a circle of eccentric friends who exposed me to everything from

Filipino stuffed grape leaves to *The Moosewood Cookbook* to the fallout of anorexia to a household where bread was baked daily with Red Fife flour delivered from Saskatchewan.

Did I learn anything in class? Not really. My education was self-directed, self-serving, mostly Vietnamese but gaining ground one durian shake at a time.

Indian Tacos with Mona

When I first met Mona Staats, I fell under her spell, just as Derek did with Tom Brown Jr. I minded my posture and my p's and q's in her presence. She was an icon and elder from the Six Nations of the Grand River, the largest First Nations Reserve in Canada (and the only reservation with all six Iroquois nations living together). Mona was in tune to a different rhythm, a beating drum from long ago and the heartbeat of Mother Nature.

I was working part-time at Apps' Mill Nature Centre cleaning punky turtle tanks, feeding the albino ferret and leading Girl Guide troops on plant identification hikes. On Sundays, the centre invited local nature celebs to speak. Mona Staats was one of our guests and as we chatted over dishwater tea and Arrowroot biscuits, I found myself agreeing to help her out that summer, in whatever capacity I could.

She needed someone with a strong back to help her plants trees and clear some trails to exact her vision of a Six Nations Wildlife Trail and Heritage Cabin. I was all in despite not having a driver's license or means of getting there aside from riding my bike (which would take nearly an hour). "I can pick you up and drive you home. And as thanks, I'll treat you to lunch. Do you like Indian tacos?"

I had no idea if I did but it seemed like a sweet deal all around. That steamy summer I'd ride one-way out to Mona's house in Ohsweken and she'd rehydrate me with gallons of sickeningly sweet iced tea upon arrival. "Let's have some strawberry shortcake before we start in on things." Mona cut generous squares of shortcake and split wild strawberries from her property into our bowls. She scooped vanilla ice cream, adding an extra scoop to mine because I had ridden so far and because I "was taller."

Mona shared the colourful legends of her people, touring me through her life and culture between each spoonful. She was unstoppable once the work began. We dug, planted, yanked weeds, bushwhacked and dragged fallen trees until we were faint from exertion. "Lunch," she'd insist. My bare legs would be scratched to shit from briars and thorns. Mona smartly wore polyester pants and looked like she was ready to attend a matinee, neatly pressed and glowing.

She introduced me to the extraordinary menu at Little Buffalo, a gas station/restaurant where Chiefswood Road crossed Indian Line.

Indian Tacos were a far cry from the stale Old El Paso crap I associated with tacos. Old El Paso corn shells shattered upon first bite, sending a confetti of hot beef, salsa and sour cream into your lap. Indian Tacos were intelligently made with a traditional fry bread, a dense flat dough that was fried or deep-fried in lard or shortening to a donut-like golden finish. Smothered with chunky, smoky chili and topped with mittfuls of shredded cheese, shredded lettuce, diced onion, and tomatoes – Indian Tacos were a teenage dream.

"Have you had corn soup?" It was made with hominy (which meant nothing to me then), a canned product of dried maize (corn) kernels treated with alkali (which makes the corn's texture mysteriously beefier). The cloudy soup was flavoured with bits of fatty pork and a mince of onion, celery, carrots and kidney beans. It was worth sacrificing my legs to the patches of poison oak and stinging nettle on Mona's property.

We lunched at Little Buffalo whenever I rode out to "work." It wasn't work at all – I loved Mona's company and knowledge. I became a total chatterbox, eager for the first-hand education she provided – a genuine "brown bag lunch" of informal learning that I swallowed whole. I asked her about smudging, sweat lodges, sweetgrass and some of the storylines that were evolving on my CBC drama *North of 60*, based on a fictional First Nations community called Lynx River. She was forever patient and there was always more corn soup.

Some days we'd slack off and go to the dump. "Shall we?" A wide grin would spread across Mona's face. "We should let our stomachs settle anyway." Back then, we could pull into the dump and go "picking," no questions asked. Mona knew I had an issue with my bike seat and found one that was more suitable for a riding lawnmower. I loved that she poked around with kid-like enthusiasm. There were always treasures to be found, and she was a treasured friend, long after that golden summer of fry bread and corn soup edged into the first frost.

I was also lunching with two teachers from the enrichment centre I attended in elementary school. Suzanne and Janice insisted I call them by their first names and I navigated clumsy lunches trying to be cool and sophisticated at Brantford's first-date-fancy Al Dente Italian restaurant. Worried about twirling myself into a fool and splattering my mentors with linguini and herbed white wine garlic butter, I often ordered the jumbo cheese ravioli with spicy vodka sauce. I was familiar with Chef Boyardee ravioli and knew it was a solid choice. Pepper was ground from a mill over my shoulder and parmesan shaved before my very eyes in cute curls. "And something to drink?"

Suzanne and Janice ordered Perrier so I followed suit. Individual bottles were brought to our table with a confident twist and elegant half pour. After my first tomato red-faced choking fit from inhaling the unknown effervescence of the sparkling water, I resumed sophisticated conversation.

I was being educated at all angles, from Mona's gourmet gas station to the elegant ladies' lunch with two women I adored. We met once a month, either at Cultures (one of the first chains to find a devout following of their salad and smoothie-centric menu) or Slingsby's, a gastropub located in a converted warehouse space along the Grand River. I became accustomed to Perrier and not putting my elbows on the table.

At Alex's house, I was introduced to several pages of *The Moosewood Cookbook*, sunflower seed butter spread on rice cakes and the virtues of vegetarianism. Who knew a pizza crust could be fabricated out of cottage cheese and spinach? We talked more often about the merits of *thirtysomething* and *My So-Called Life*. Alex and I were both silently looking forward to the launch out of high school and twentysomething.

Alex's mom was my English teacher and a brilliant force. She bought me a copy of *The Songlines* by Bruce Chatwin, recognizing early on that I was growing eager to explore my own nomadic travels. My focus had turned to moving to Australia (because, why not?) and she thought Chatwin's purposeful mission of researching Aboriginal song might inspire me to identify a greater purpose beyond just "moving to Australia."

Proudly, I asked Joan to come to "my" Quan 99. She was gracious and took it all in with grace. She too was charmed by the tiny family at the back watching cartoons and the curious and addictive soursop shakes. She questioned me about "this Antoine fellow" who had convinced me to move to Australia with him. We met at an outdoor leadership camp on Bark Lake and for the next year planned craft-focussed weekends at his house in Warkworth and tie-dye T-shirt production at mine (because my family had a washer and dryer and his didn't). Antoine's life floored me – his mom made bread from scratch every day. Honey came from the hives out back. His dad bottled a mead that left us all a little tipsy after bowls of chilled cucumber soup one early summer day. Chilled cucumber soup! Wine made out of honey!

Sometimes we met halfway, in Toronto. Antoine's brother, Georg, was a uni student who lived in the west end and we "crashed" as teens do, on his parquet living floor in a lumpy array of blankets and afghans on an even lumpier makeshift mattress of couch cushions. By day, Antoine and I poked around Chinatown eating spicy pork buns, custardy egg tarts and spongy lotus pancakes. He expertly bought starfruit and dragon fruit just because. These things were not generally stocked in the fruit and veg sections of Warkworth or Brantford grocers and Antoine was undaunted. Both the starfruit and dragon fruit tasted like slices of mothballs, but this was entry-level exotica for me.

In the company of Bob Vamos, it was all about thieving the just-baked chocolate chip cookies from the high school cafeteria. The staff would be occupied stirring vats of muddy gravy and boiling endless macaroni noodles. In a rush of wrongdoing and temptation, Bob and I would dash through the open door, grab three or four cookies and squeal out of the caf, running to the safety of our lockers like bank robbers. Yeah, I should probably send Brantford Collegiate Institute about thirty-six dollars for stolen cookies.

Bob was famous for not wanting to break a loonie, so I ponied up the coins for our legit purchases, which often took the form of salty fries with beefy gravy. He also didn't like to break a two-dollar bill or five for that matter. We'd split fries or a beef-a-roni special, even though we both had packed lunches from home.

Thanks to my Filipino friend Moiz, I learned the delicate art of stuffing grape leaves with rice and fresh mint under the tutelage of his soft-spoken father. This guy pan-fried naked zucchini into a soft and sumptuous dish that I couldn't get enough of. In our household, zucchini was promptly disguised inside a chocolate loaf – it was never a stand alone and if it were, it would have stood alone all night on my plate.

Penny and I bonded over after school McCain curly fries and her crazy playlist of The Jesus and the Mary Chain and Pixies. Jen Blackett and I had clove-breathed confessionals over soup bowl-sized servings of Bengal Spice Celestial Tea listening to the rallying cries of Buffy Sainte-Marie and folky comfort of Neil Young. Emily showed her gratitude for my poster-making efforts in her "Em for Students' Council

Secretary" campaign via secret chicken finger and plum sauce lunches at the local golf and country club on her parents' account.

With Jeremy, my Snakmaster partner in crime, and Evan, his partner in crime, it was a reliable Friday night feed at Taco Bell on King George Road. For two bucks we had ten tacos to go and, if Evan had his flirting way with the doe-eyed drive-thru gal, we'd land a free order of Fries Supreme with a hot mess of seasoned beef, salsa, cheese and a puff of sour cream. Conversation wasn't necessary largely due to the *Reservoir Dogs* soundtrack Paul pumped out of his Volvo speakers at a level that made the tacos crack. While Evan and Jeremy fought for the fourth taco, Paul thoughtfully ate his cold Eat to Win boiled potato and Derek smoked a Camel, his mind set on surviving in the wild with a knife and maybe just a little tobacco for good measure.

Taco Bell was a far cry from Little Buffalo's Indian Tacos. Alex's *Moosewood Cookbook* pizza with cottage cheese (which I only knew as a lasagna layer pre-Alex) was a further cry from sticky, gingery duck wings with her mom at Quan 99, but it was an inadvertent education in petty crime, Indigenous history, Chinatown, fast food and slow talk with the friends who kindly invited me to their tables.

Minister of Nutrition

It still seems like fake news to me. How I was voted into a chapter of the Ontario Secondary School Student Association's (OSSSA) cabinet as the "Minister of *Nutrition*" is laughable. Me! Minister of Nutrition! It was no big secret that a plate of cafeteria fries with gravy and a wading pool of European bougie mayo dip was my routine go-to. Me! The one who voluntarily mowed through a month of Rosa's pepperoni pizza slices as part of a bet.

On weekends at Apps' Mill, when I worked with Greg, a very sturdy forestry student at Sir Sandford Fleming, I held my ground and matched his usual footlong and fries order from The Hitching Post. He weighed at least seventy-five pounds more than I did. After lunch, I studied bird and wildflower guides while sipping on a coffee mug filled to the brim with pure maple syrup sourced from the nature centre's grove along Whiteman's Creek.

Nutrition didn't figure large in my world. Despite familial skinny genes, I did honest legwork playing on three soccer teams, volleyball in the off-season and running track and cross-country. I joined BCI's 100-mile club on the side. I also missed the school bus a lot, which meant a ten-kilometre walk home along the train tracks.

Nan Torti still pressed, "And how much do you weigh now?" as though I were a prizefighter trying to sweat out a kilo to edge my way into a lighter class. Nan took on an unofficial role as my running coach, dog-whistling and hollering over the crowds at every race finish line.

Nan Chapin was still weighing and measuring the younger cousins at holiday gatherings but for those of us who had moved onto high school, there was a free unspoken pass to not willingly participate in favour of being cool and/ or indignant.

I wish I could explain my role as Minister of Nutrition, but I can't. I didn't even weigh in. Shortly after assuming the position, I slept the next two months away under the heavy-eye-lidded influence of mono. I'd had mono (the "kissing disease") the last month of grade eight even though I was monogamous and had only French-kissed Robert LeBovic. He graduated with the class and was relatively unscathed after kissing me.

As Minister, I *should* have been organizing the catering company and menu options for Dream '92, a three-day OSSSA leadership conference for high school students in our region. Instead, I slept like I was drugged and awoke for glugs of Snapple iced tea or whatever I was enthusiastic enough to eat. I lost my appetite and couldn't stay awake long enough for a bowl of chicken noodle soup (which was always associated with sickness in our house. Ginger ale to settle your stomach and chicken noodle soup if you were having the shits, barfs or anything related to that).

My pal Sally ended up taking over my duties, visiting me often, taking a seat at the end of my heated waterbed. She brought me frosted strawberry Pop-Tarts for consolation, filled me in on all the necessary gossip and I went back to bed until March.

But I *was* Minister of Nutrition and nobody can take that away from me.

That summer, revived by the tilt in the equinox and the end of the dismal school year, I was introduced to the sophistication of the "Three Blob Lunch" at a visual arts camp in Haliburton. This kind of nutrition spoke to me. Each nourishing blob was basically mayo with an additive that created the "salad": egg, potato or tuna.

Three blobs and a loaf of white bread were delivered to each table by the counsellors of Camp Walden. I loved the simplicity and it was my ideal Michelin 3-star entree, devoured with

DEET-scented hands under the rising chant between cabins and campers: "There ain't no flies on us!"

By age sixteen, I had yet to master egg salad sandwiches or blobs as Kiley and Dax will attest. I was more famous for egg salad "over easy." I never boiled the eggs long enough, for fear of them turning blue. Once they were peeled, split and mashed with a fork, there was no turning back. The runny yolk never fully blended with mayo to hide my blunder. My egg salad sandwiches *dripped*. (I now know my mom's secret: Bring water to a boil, slip eggs in and boil for twelve minutes. Drain. Soak in cold water for ten minutes. The eggs will be perfect every single time.)

Despite being a Minister, I had little kitchen prowess. I could blend a velvety banana shake in the Oster (one banana, ice, milk, teaspoon of vanilla, whir) and had recently added half-assed chickpea burgers potent with garlic cloves to my skinny repertoire.

I had decided to become a vegetarian because, why not? Going to Australia, going vegetarian and getting inked was all part of the random and reckless teenage agenda.

Somehow (and I'm blaming it on vegetarianism) I became part of what my mother deemed to be a Ponzi scheme with a biology teacher at our high school. I found myself rather bored but receptive to the possibility as I was connected to the owner of a supplements company in California. I think I was going to be a vitamin sales rep tapping into the niche student market but I was also just coming off my mono jetlag, so a lot of vital info was lost in my REM cycles. My mom had a hushed talk with my dad and they asked if I needed money for something. My questionable behaviour was probably eerily similar to all the telltale signs of drug abuse provided in brochures for concerned parents. In the end, they would give me the cash if I said no to my lucrative sales rep position with the dude in California.

I was easily swayed, took their money and invested in some thrift store cowboy boots and a copy of *The Vegetarian Cookbook* from my bio teacher after taking a hard pass on the supplements gig. My parents only pushed vitamins on us once. They were cutesy grape-flavoured Flintstone vitamins, shaped like Dino and Fred and the gang. We fed them all to Xanadu, who usually coughed them up like a furball but tried, tried again to swallow them. I'm sure there were a few thrown-up Fred heads lost in the shag carpet over the years.

Being a vegetarian was easy, provided I was invited over to Alex's place for dinner. I could only prepare chickpea burgers so many nights at home. The effort! The patties only remained glued together with enormous amounts of ketchup and mustard. I tried dressing the burgs up with tartar sauce, HP and pickled beets. I felt a lot like Billy in *How to Eat Fried Worms*. I smiled wistfully at old photos of Xanadu and me. For most of 1984 and 1985 I could be seen on my

BMX wearing an Ontario Pork-issued T-shirt: "Put pork on your fork. Try a little tenderness." It was my power shirt. I did not have a similar tee featuring a chickpea burger.

My vegetarianism was as short-lived as Debbie Gibson's singing career and acid-wash jeans. My mom was confident that I could stunt my growth by being a stubborn vegetarian. Under her tutelage, I terminated my downhill ways at Admiral Submarine on Dalhousie Street. Jeremy and the guys called it Gus's and Gus may have been the owner, the cook or some inside joke that I can't recall. Regardless, Admiral's was reliable for greasy good burgers and chip wagon-style fries and I suppose submarines. The place was designed for hangovers. A regular hamburger came with two patties that left your lips slippery with fat. Anyone over the age of twenty-five felt confident in knowing that the closest defibrillator was six minutes away at the Brantford General Hospital.

There was not a hint of chickpea in a Gus burger and I went back to "the other side" without shamefully looking back. The grass was greener on the other side because of those cows!

Being a vegetarian involved more sacrifice than my teen brain could handle. I was already sacrificing good portions of my day by going to high school. I didn't have time to create meal plans or meals for that matter with all my extra-curriculars and sleeping.

Was it worth giving up my mom's juicy bone-in pork chops sweetened with a heavy ladle of Nan Torti's cinnamon-flecked Northern Spy applesauce? Mindless handfuls of Frito Baken-Ets Pork Rinds would be off the table too. Gone: my mom's bacon and cheese broiler buns; Sunday roast beef sandwiches on a buttered Kaiser with a smear of horseradish and squeeze of mustard. Farewell fork tines wound tight with starchy noodles and beefy spaghetti sauce. Bye turkey gravy running like lava from the volcanic mound of mashed potatoes thickened with whole fat sour cream. I couldn't imagine the absence of hot and crispy Kentucky Fried Chicken skin laden with the secret eleven herbs and spices packed into my cheeks like chewing tobacco. Adieu to my grandfather's gamey moose burgers sauced in ketchup and those lovely oily pepperoni rounds on steaming stretchy cheese slices from Rosa's.

I wasn't ready for the absence of all my major food groups, from fried smelts to slop, in one go. And as fast as my Australian whims turned due west to Vancouver, my affection for chickpea burgers turned to 100 percent beef.

I can hear Grandma's scratchy cackle now, a rolling patchy laugh that revealed her seven dedicated decades of smoking cigarettes. "Vegetarian? Why in Sam Hill would you do that? You'll stunt your growth. And you'll probably get worms."

I realized then that my mom's playbook was a shared and dog-eared one, borrowed from the family tree library. The oral history of superstitions, old wives' tales and convoluted theories had trickled down from my great-great grandmother Alice Sophia Franklin to my great-grandmother Grace Evelyn Arthur to my grandmother Joyce Yvonne Chapin to my mom, Sandra Elaine Torti. To me, Julie Kathleen Torti.

Amazing Grace

"Why don't you come in, take a look around. It sure is different! That ol' black and white checkered linoleum is long gone!" Judy said.

Judy was the effervescent mom of my rival high school-era friend, Nikki, who I played soccer and volleyball against from midget to senior league.

Judy had bought my great-grandmother's house a few years previous and insisted that my mom and I come in for a snoop. I hadn't been "home" in a year and my parents had moved from our childhood house into the city. Whenever Kiley and I were in the province my mom liked to toot us out to our old stomping grounds. We'd cruise past our elementary school in Mount Pleasant, past my grandparents' pig farm on the corner and slow to see what changes the new owners had made to our house. The tamaracks and pines my parents had planted in the former orchard seemed to double in size each visit. The walnut trees that lined Grandma's laneway were living skyscrapers.

I had moved to the Fraser Valley in British Columbia in the summer of 2007 and made Toronto a layover in my awkward flight path to Lubumbashi, Congo. I was going to be flying for nearly twenty-four hours anyway so I arranged a leg from Abbotsford, B.C., to Toronto and a week later, onward to Amsterdam, Nairobi, Harare and Lubumbashi.

My mom was white-knuckled about it all. Even though she was driving, I'm sure it was all a blur and Judy's sudden appearance at the side of the road was like an apparition. Distractions were welcome at this point. I understood. No mother should be comfortable with their daughter striking off to the Congo to make breakfast for chimpanzees at a zoo, but that's exactly what I was doing. Even though I never woke up in time to have breakfast myself.

Seeing the neat patchwork of the vegetable gardens, I smirked in memory of Grandma calling us orangutans. At the time, we had no idea what they were but she insisted our unruly behaviour was exactly like them. She often threatened to "skin us alive" for good reason and if we were too hyper, she likened us to "a bunch of 'rangutans." Funny that I should end up working with primates – perhaps her name-calling was a foreshadowing. I would later learn that a bunch of orangutans is actually called a "congress" or "buffoonery." She was onto something.

"Do you want to go in and see the house?" my mom asked, unsure.

There was a pause in my response. Yes. No? Did I want to keep my visuals of Grandma's house intact? What if seeing Judy's modern renos erased my original version of that familiar black and white checker lino and the ever-present bar of Zest soap on the pedestal sink? Curiosity ate away at me. "Yes, let's do it."

My mom wheeled down the laneway, tennis ball-sized green walnuts pressed out of their shells under the weight of the car tires. The smell was unforgettable – like bergamot. If you whipped enough of them at your brutish cousin's head, the aftermath left your hands stained and scented like Earl Grey tea.

The trees stood like sentries. They were still there but Grandma wasn't.

In grade three, when our class had to illustrate our family tree on construction paper, I couldn't believe that Grandma's branch sprouted in 1907. Nan Torti's branch budded in 1924 while Nan and Grandpa followed in 1930 and 1931. My family tree was rather lopsided, but the roots remained strong and the branches were full of colourful birds.

It was nearly impossible to comprehend a time void of frosted strawberry Pop-Tarts and *The Jetsons*. *Little House on the Prairie* was the closest we came to understanding what Grandma's wrinkles had seen. She had been widowed in 1968 and was as tough as the Canadian Shield, never marrying again. Grandma died on October

12, 1997, at age ninety and her house became Judy's.

As Judy proudly swanned around the house, my brain did double-time downloading the new images while comparing the old files. The house was in dire need of an update but updating nostalgia is a different beast to contend with. There were no brilliant blue and lime green budgies singing away. The guppy tank with the sunken treasure buried in the flamingo pink pebble-bottom wasn't bubbling in the corner. Sam, Grandma's fat white cat, wasn't curling figure eights around our ankles. There were no porcelain black panthers or vases filled with peacock feathers and wheat sheaves. The frog that held the gummy dish sponge was long gone, in favour of sleek, contemporary design. The salt and pepper shaker cabinet that held over a hundred sets was absent. So was the ever-present crystal glass bowl of giant pink candies the size of the driveway walnuts that we all gagged on. All of this had been blotted out with hardwood, stainless steel and marble, rendering "Grandma" a stranger. Could I still detect the perfume of puffball slices frying in butter in her cast iron pan? Oily and savoury rabbit stew simmering on the backburner? Yes.

I rattled off the memories as they filtered in. "This is where the chocolate or jelly cake rolls were kept." I explained to Judy how we would gingerly unroll them like magic carpets and lick the icing or jelly from the cake. "She always had tins of pull-tab chocolate pudding and Del Monte fruit cups for us too." The "fruit" cups that were 100 percent liquid invert sugar with 1/18th of a maraschino cherry in each cup.

"Here, oh my god, when Grandma got on the party phone line, we'd crack open the fridge and fill our throats with endless aerosol whipped cream." My mom rarely bought the stuff so Grandma's Reddi-wip was a hot item until one of us had a snorting coughing fit, blowing the cover (and snot) on our covert operation.

I indicated where the chest freezer was as it was a landmark battleground for TV dinners on Friday nights. It was cut-throat between Kiley and me for the fried chicken or hot turkey dinner. Dax was always pleased with the Salisbury steak feature, but the fried chicken was worthy of a hair-pulling, pinching and biting war until tears.

My mom took in the changes silently. She had seen many more evolutions of the farmhouse than I had. Judy interrupted our time capsule as we leaned into the primary bedroom. "You know, she still visits us. I can hear her cough now and again."

Grandma's signature sandpaper cough was proof of the three-packs-a-day cigarette habit she established shortly after the age of twelve. Dax, Kiley and I can thank her for extinguishing any interest in smoking, ever.

Tobacco was Grandma's lifeblood. I wasn't surprised that her ghost coughed. My great-grandfather, who died from a heart attack in 1968 (six years before I was born), bought the farm from his father back in 1938. Then, the eleven-acre lot had three tobacco kilns, two orchards and a greenhouse. Tobacco was sold in Delhi (forty-five minutes from Mount Pleasant) for nineteen cents a pound. Talk about up in smoke! My mother's genealogy archives show that one hundred pounds of turnips or potatoes sold for twenty-five cents that same year. I think my great-grandparents coined the term "subsistence agriculture." It was purely for survival with zero surplus or frills to brag about.

I stood at the front window of Judy's kitchen drinking in the unchanged view of the tobacco kilns across the road. The smell of tobacco curing can't be forgotten. It's sweet, sensual and the kind of smell that makes you inhale like yoga instructors encourage. Like it's your last breath, lungs like helium balloons in the confines of your rib cage.

We thanked Judy for the tour and left the old farm with minds busier than beehives after the unexpected step back in time.

For anyone who has worked on a farm, the mixed feelings are a troubled stew, save for the mid-life crisis "farmers" of late who have sold their Toronto manses for a small acreage to grow lavender as a whimsical hobby.

At age nine, my mother was in her second year as a "boat unloader" on her dad's tobacco farm. When she was tall enough, she graduated to "leaf handler." Both jobs were backbreaking and full of sacrifice. She never wanted us to endure that same hardship even though farming was deep in the maternal and paternal family veins from County Derry in Northern Ireland and Weymouth in southern England to halcyon Mount Pleasant township in Ontario.

Her stories of my great-grandfather's threshing machines operated by steam engine and hay wagons pulled by Belgian horses are unfathomable. He grew hay, rye, wheat and a local unofficial farmer's collective (ten broad-chested men or so) would get together and go to each other's farm come harvest. There were always hired hands and the tobacco growers would sleep in a bunkie out by the tobacco kilns as they were coal-fired back then and fire was an ever-present risk. Many workers were relatives or locals, and because transportation was an issue, residing on the farm made sense. The farmers were required to feed their help and do their laundry. It was an all-inclusive without the beach time and volleyball in the pool.

Grandma's all-inclusive featured homemade elderberry wine, though I was too young to ever have a nip. She canned everything for survival, not hobby. Peaches, pears, apples, cherries, strawberries, blueberries and elderberries were all preserved for the daunting winter ahead. No wonder Grandma's hands were so knotted with arthritis. In her later years she often blamed her "sleeping hands" for dropped dishes. Finally, her hands could rest.

Amazing Grace Arthur. Thank you for the fish eyes and feeding the buffoonery of orangutans.

Living Off the Land

In contrast to my chronicles and confessions of a very preservative-laden and sugar-coated childhood, we did live off the land in equal measure. We were self-sufficient and growing our own menu long before it became an Instagram hashtag and millennial trend.

My Grandma's garden was Dax's pipe dream (minus the pipe and tobacco). His market garden was a well-curated design of companion planting. He knew to grow tomatoes, peppers and carrots together. He knew not to plant peas near the onions and potatoes well away from his twelve-foot-tall sunflowers. Dax introduced the family to composting thirty-five years ago.

He was only eight when he begged my mom to borrow my grandfather's rototiller. That first year, he was still too tiny for the monster pull of the rototiller – even my dad was a wet noodle in its wake. Initially, there was a knee-jerk reaction from my dad about "ruining the grass" and if the garden initiative tanked, he knew he'd have a lot of seeding and fertilizing to return it to its royal state. My dad still loves his grass (not *that* kind). He is meticulous about it and never trusted the "whipper snipper" to do the same finesse job that he could do on his hands and knees with gritted teeth. For years we only had a push mower for two acres of grass. As soon as Dax could safely sit in the saddle, he wanted to assume grass cutting duties because it was quick coin and the most lucrative chore on offer at our house. Kiley and I were okay with simply begging for money and making empty promises about doing dishes more often in the future. Right.

In the dead of winter, Dax composed his seed order from the Stokes catalogue while Kiley and I carefully completed multiple choice questionnaires in *Tiger Beat* magazine. Was I totally compatible with River Phoenix? Was I his dream girlfriend material or Kiley? How much did we really know about Kirk Cameron's secret life? Was his curly hair all-natural?

What I really knew about Dax's garden was that he produced bright jewels of raspberries bigger than thimbles. It was best to wait for him to pick them as the wicked thorns grabbed at your bare skin and would pull a T-shirt clean from your shoulders.

Dax grew a healthy row of thumb-sized asparagus, willowy dill, burgundy beets as big as croquet balls, perfect radish globes, wonky pumpkins and giant cukes. He'd confidently try new varieties, heirlooms and, once, popcorn. It grew just like regular sweet corn with the exception of the longer harvest time (when the husks browned). Dax grew peanuts, crazy carrots and giant strawberries – single-handed. He'd trade off surplus with Nan Chapin, who always went overboard in her zucchini production. "You have to take some." She pushed them on us like party drugs, which may explain the constant loaves of chocolate zucchini bread on our counter.

Smartly, Dax sold this produce back to my parents (to account for his labour and re-search). In the off-season Dax baked sweets for my friends and sold them too. I remember my mom's jaw dropping when Camille handed Dax a crisp hundred-dollar bill for a few dozen Nanaimo bars and a dense chocolate chip cheese-cake with Oreo crust. At that time (and still), Dax failed to account for the pricey ingredients that my mom purchased for his part-time catering gig.

I was still happy eating footlongs with Greg and feeding the albino ferret at the nature centre for a steady weekend income while Kiley came home smelling exactly like a coffee pot after her evening shifts at Tim Hortons.

I'm surprised Dax didn't get into canning because he could have tripled his profit. Instead, after cooking for a half-dozen palliative care cli-ents during the day, my mom would come home and cook for us and preserve Dax's bounty on the weekend. (River Phoenix and Kirk Cameron made no mention of looking for a girlfriend with a garden or someone who knew how to make Nanaimo bars – or pickled beets for that matter. Kiley and I made note of that.)

My mom's sweet pickled beets would disappear as soon as they were jarred and set. Exhausted, she'd pour a glass of cabernet sauvignon the same colour as the disappeared beets and weep inside, I'm sure. Her dill pickles vanished just as quickly in crisp, sour bites that would cramp our jaws. She made bread and butters too, with perfect pinches of allspice, cloves and celery seeds. Her strawberry and raspberry jams were made the old-school way by pouring hot paraffin over the prepared jam. Whoever was lucky enough to open a new jar had dibs on plucking the hardened wax puck out and licking it like a lollipop.

We relied on Grandma for her garlicky pickled yellow and green beans that would stand in jars like soldiers. Nan Torti was known for her trio: peach jam, super sweet beets (that I adored) and velvety, smooth as a baby's butt applesauce. Nan was particular about her apples and was exclusive – only Northern Spies from Bennett's Apples in Ancaster would do. She respected their quality, taste profile, snappy bite and bushel price point. Plus, Bennett's was within the radius of an ooey-gooey Cinnabon fix. It was win-win.

The '80s and '90s signalled the end of a tremendously delicious era right down to the unavoidable association with "Weird Al" Yankovic's

1984 Grammy Award-winning "Eat It." Even markers smelled like food. Mr. Sketch marketed a scented marker line with intoxicating smells like licorice (my favourite marker to inhale), cinnamon, lemon, grape, apple and watermelon. Mr. Sketch markers, remarkably, are still available for purchase because, according to the company and consumers, nothing beats the union of colour and scent. Teachers never understood that winning concept. I can still hear the hush instilled after Miss Dutton's final hot-faced warning to the culprits (me): "Stop smelling your markers!"

Luckily, when grounded from marker huffing, we had scratch-and-sniff stickers to breathe in.

In grade three, anyone who was cool had a sticker book and next to "puffies" and "shinies" the "smelly stickers" were the coveted collection. My root beer and dill pickle stickers were a favourite go-to and long after the image of the glass of root beer and pickle was erased by an aggressive scratchy nail, the smell remained. How is it that Dolce & Gabbana's Light Blue cologne has a fraction of dill pickle scratch-and-sniff sticker smell life?

Kiley had a set of Strawberry Shortcake dolls that never stopped smelling either, after years of brushing their hair and several hundred tea parties with Xanadu. These dolls were a great temptation to Dax and me. Instead of Miss Dutton's alarm cry it was Kiley's: "Stop smelling my Purple Pie Man!" He was the best whiff. And

Lemon Meringue, with her corn silk hair that smelled exactly like a gently squeezed Meyer.

All the best things seemed to have a smell that lingered for unnatural amounts of time. I'm not talking about farts, either. I mean, those French fry boxes we "accidentally" kicked under the seats of the Pinto turned the vehicle into a deep fryer and vinegar bottle overnight.

Our preferred food groups stained our faces and fingers for a solid eight hours: Welch's grape juice, ketchup chips, blue freezies, Doritos. The most exceptional foods could also be classified by the level they packed up on your teeth or caused internal injury.

Cap'n Crunch, Corn Pops and Styrofoam-textured sour cream and onion rings did the trick for adding height to your molars. On the top of the proceed-with-caution list, Nan Chapin's pincushion chow mein-riddled haystack cookies. Close on the heels of her cookies: blind handfuls of General Mills Bugles or Fritos corn chips. Curled just the right way, or crunched the wrong way, both could perforate the roof of your mouth faster than a pit viper's strike. Also on the lethal front: Chicken Bones candy. For those of us who patiently sucked on the rectangular hot cinnamon hard candy until it turned into a thin candy razor inside your mouth, you'll know. The slow suck to access the skinny chocolate-plugged centre was never worth the wait. The bone always went down your throat sideways. Always. Like a darning needle. Like a chicken bone.

Just as the smelly markers, stickers and doll hair scent lasted several decades, some aftertastes lasted equally long. Case in point: All-dressed chips. They'd dress your tongue in a flavour funk that would resist two earnest teeth-brushing sessions. In the longevity category, somehow the smell of a Burger King Whopper could remain on your hands for just as long – even after a thorough lather with Irish Spring. Even a burp twelve hours post-Whopper tasted like you'd just swallowed your last bite. "Hurry, get the Gaviscon for Buffer!"

All these years later I still wonder how a Kentucky Fried Chicken location can permeate the air a full kilometre away. Like a skunk. I can't smell KFC without thinking of Nan Torti and her chicken skin donation when we picnicked. Kiley, Dax and I went into beast mode with claws out. Meanwhile, Nan quietly abided by her diet, picking at a flavourless skinned breast, eating coleslaw with her hair pick without complaint because Buffer forgot to grab cutlery.

Childhood was definitely the ideal time to focus on sugar, saturated fats and making Juicy Fruit gum wrapper chains. It was a precious period of time when eating junk food like Cracker Jack's caramel corn or junky cereal was rewarded with a congratulatory prize. Drinking Kool-Aid and sucking on Popsicles was fruitful – we collected hundreds of UPC codes and Popsicle sticks in a valiant race to win "1 of 1,000" Kool-Aid beach towels or a crappy Hostess Munchie pill box hat with flaps.

I haven't touched ninety percent of what I've waxed on about since my saccharine youth for dozens of reasons that have everything to do with health, wellness and a permanent retainer behind my lower front teeth. Retainers are not symbiotic with sticky Kraft caramels, those neatly wrapped Halloween-issue Kerr's molasses taffy kisses or a misguided bite of the granite sugar shell of a candy apple.

I'm okay with not eating any of those things anymore, really. The craving seems greatest when it's taboo, doesn't it? Or in the instance when the craving becomes primal – when you've eaten nothing but clumpy rice and farty black beans and greasy canned mackerel for three months. I confess to swallowing two Burger King Whoppers in quick succession when I exited the Costa Rican jungles in February 1995 (I'm blaming the worms. I was eating for a thousand!) – but I haven't had one since.

Human bodies are constantly seeking homeostasis, balance. There's a reason why we crave things – even wild parrots in Peru will lick riverbank cliffs for the minerals they are lacking. In my thirties, I witnessed Ugandans purchasing "dirt" at the market – to eat. Pregnant and lactating women in Africa can replenish nutritional needs by eating clay. "Geophagy" is the practice of eating earth, differing greatly from my own sour key cravings.

"You'll get cankers!" Nan Torti promised us as we sucked the salt crystals from gummy sour keys and sour worms with crossed eyes and cramping masseter muscles. She was right but we didn't help matters by licking our way through a bag of Hostess salt and vinegar chips. We came by it naturally. Desperate, when my mom was a kid, the salt blocks that were placed in the fields for the pigs and horses were her reasonable facsimile for a bag of salt and vinegar chips. She'd surreptitiously run through the pastures to get her sodium licks in before dinner.

My mom wasn't too far off in her search for salt and maybe my misguided geophagy (misinterpreted as the practice of eating nothing but cholesterol, palm oils, artificial colours, BHT, sulfite, partially hydrogenated oils and high fructose corn syrup) was successfully satisfied after two decades of focussed intake. I had my bout with worms, just as my mother promised, and was cured.

It's a miracle, really. I can see myself pilfering sugar cubes from the "cafeteria" at Mount Pleasant Public, where the teachers kept their coffee supplies. I ate them like a happy horse, letting them dissolve on my tongue just like my mom and her giant salt cube.

Back then, a day wasn't complete without a Swiss Roll, Pop-Tart, Tahiti Treat, cream soda or Vachon Super Passion raspberry pastry. Better yet, all of the above. Followed up by a spongy Vachon Ah Caramel! while listening to some INXS. My diary entries read like love letters to Dairy Queen. I sometimes wonder if I played soccer and ran cross-country just for the Oreo blizzard or tricoloured Firecracker Popsicle at the finish line. There's no doubt that my parents wondered if my fame would come in the form of winning Nathan's Hot Dog Eating Contest. (Note: Miki Sudo, the defending women's champion, ate forty-eight and a half hot dogs in 2020. Joey Chestnut, in the men's division, ate seventy-five.)

I get full too fast. I'm a loser at buffets because there's no way I could fathom four hot dogs, let alone forty-eight. My most successful food competition didn't involve eating at all. In grade nine I beat out a senior linebacker in the not-so-flattering Chubby Bunny competition. I managed to stuff eighteen marshmallows (not the mini version) in my mouth. I credit my orthodontist with this win as I had my mouth cranked open and packed full of gauze like a weird Christmas turkey for the removal of four molars for braces and then another four wisdom teeth.

Chubby bunny.

That's what you had to say after you added another marshmallow to the mix.

Not my best work.

I had no desire to enter eating competitions after seeing my Chubby Bunny yearbook photo. I had no burning desire to enter the food industry in any capacity, really, but I was still intrigued by it. Meanwhile, Kiley was scooping ice cream during the summers at West End, doing something vital in the bakery at the local grocery store on weekends in addition to pouring coffee at Tim Hortons. Dax was still smartly self-employed, tending to his garden, baking extravagant cheesecakes, avoiding union fee deductions and workplace politics.

In my twenties, I had irrational ideas about becoming a sommelier (after a summer of drinking homemade merlot and Blue Nun) or a food critic. I was living in a town with three chicken wing joints and a take-out pizza place. What could I critique? Chocolatier? I didn't even eat chocolate anymore but if we're comparing experience credentials, Kiley never drank a cup of coffee or baked a thing.

My food industry ambitions dissolved as quickly as a TUMS tablet.

Dear Diary: You won't believe it now, but when you're thirty-five, you're gonna make breakfast for chimpanzees in the Congo and order goat testicles for dinner. I never dreamed that my eating résumé would grow to include line-caught piranhas and fried grasshoppers, but it did.

How to Eat Fried Grasshoppers

Fast-forward twenty years to 2021. The sound-track in my home is nearly identical to what was cranked out of Kiley's boombox decades before (yes, Tiffany, still). Outside of my stalled playlist, I've become a crazy patchwork of the people and places that have influenced me in forty-six years. I've gleaned the best (and worst) of everyone's habits and traditions from Banff to the Congo.

I have a small arsenal of recipes that jump from Grandma's dandelion wine to my west coast roomie's bannock to a piquant fish sauce that I begged off of Paule, an effervescent housekeeper at our hotel in the Seychelles in 2020. My spice rack now has saffron from Zanzibar, Gibby's steak spice from Montreal and coarse sea salt laced with rosemary. Surprisingly, there's no taxidermy-in-wait in the freezer – mostly because my dozens of bagels hog all the real estate.

I've blended in my wife's favourites, specialties (eggs Benny and cranberry turkey burgs) and merged her mother's staples: mustard pickles, sticky spareribs, even stickier sweet & sour meatballs, salt cod cakes and wafer-thin "ranger cookies" pockmarked with Rice Krispies. Kim and I both have recipes from exes that live on despite the long-expired relationships. Thank you to those we loved before for the balsamic and cumin vinaigrette served on rocket greens with candied walnuts; wilted rapini with balsamic, pan-fried chickpeas with caramelized onions and torn prosciutto; chunky chili unexpectedly sweetened with brown sugar. Long after the exciting, snappy flavour of our past relationships grew stale, a few recipes remained as legacies.

We've poached Kim's sister's dill pickle soup recipe (though we prefer when she makes it for us) and our Maritime friend Noelle's seductive white wine and garlic sauce for Malpeque Bay mussels. From my mom: her orzo salad with briny slivers of kalamata olives and summer sweet sun-dried tomatoes. Both of her Caesar salad dressings are a summer necessity. Creamy or vinaigrette? Kim always votes for the mayo-laden creamy version.

To be truthful, I farm out a lot of recipes to my mom, still. *Can you make this when we come?* Our bag of sugar is reserved for the hummingbird feeder from May until October. Flour? I think I've bought one bag in my life. Luckily, from that one bag of flour I made *Chatelaine* ginger molasses cookies for my parents and my mom latched on to the recipe and continues to make them – while I do not. Many thanks to *Chatelaine* for those spicy gingers and the rich French onion soup recipe that goes into circulation every winter. I do have a copy of Dax's "Betty's Bread Pizza" from his 4-H course but have yet to make it. How can I compete? And again, flour!

For Kim and me, our collective grown-up kitchen has become a turnstile of "Today's Specials" from all of our combined yesterdays. This blackboard of indelible chalk amalgamates our previous lives, travels and grandmothers in crazy zigzags connecting everything we've eaten from Kim's mother's "poor man's pizza" to fried calamari in Greece to our shared blackened barracuda bites in Belize to Mexican cachaça caipirinhas with a heavy squeeze of lime and chance.

When my former spa boss sold her Leslieville house and decamped to Mérida, Mexico, with her husband to open a boutique hotel, Kim and I ended up with all their fridge condiments as we were the last stop before they headed to YYZ (Toronto's Pearson International Airport) to kickstart their dream. It's ironic that two devout vegans would be the ones to introduce us to hickory-flavoured liquid smoke. Don't tell the vegans – Kim has integrated it into her beef burgers and the secret smoke addition is the umami!

It's people. Places. The caipirinhas *and* coffees and Caesars (cocktails and salads).

Vancouver. Toronto. Abbotsford, B.C. Toronto. Uganda. Congo. Toronto. West Galt. Uxbridge. Lion's Head. Like every couple, we become a mixing bowl of everything we've tasted, spat out, ruined and loved.

My Vancouver-era kitchen (circa 1993) was an unpredictable menu of dumpster diving finds and desperate twists on ramen noodles. Melted cinnamon hearts replaced sugar in cups of dishwater tea, diluted from recycling Tetley Orange Pekoe bags just one more time. During that slim and starved sojourn, I discovered full-bodied garam masala and carob chips courtesy of my hippie roomies. I tasted the fermented *POW!* of oolichan thanks to another temporary Tsimshian First Nations guest from Prince Rupert, B.C.

In turn, I swapped mugs of velvety General Foods International Coffees (ooh la la, French Vanilla Café and Suisse Mocha!) from Nan Torti's care packages for oily oolichan and bloated, boiled perogies with margarine. Our household lived on powdered coffees, starch and fermented fish (and Fleetwood Mac), warding off the penetrating damp west coast winter with the oven on BROIL (and the oven door wide open).

I blew my slim freelance paycheque (four hundred bucks a month) on fancy Flying Wedge Pizza slices in Kitsilano. The "Aphrodite" veggie triangles were loaded with feel-good garlicky eggplant, zucchini and marinated artichoke hearts. I treated myself to silken Fraser Valley chocolate milk in glass bottles, justifying the money I saved on sugar (by using cinnamon hearts as sweeteners) and eating thirty-three-cent spicy shrimp-flavoured ramen.

Shifting from my boho Vancouver chapter to philanthropy, I signed up for a three-month volunteer stint in Costa Rica, which helped confirm the reality of reality TV and the food fantasies that *Survivor* contestants weep over. My jungle diary (circa 1994) is a sobbing tribute to the unmatchable beauty of a Burger King Whopper, my mom's moist lemon-lime poke cake and carrot cake buttercream frosting. I talk about McDonald's Chicken McNuggets dunked in thick plum sauce in a lexicon more appropriate for a Harlequin novel. Deep in the soggy rainforest, I wrote near-poetry about the virtues of movie theatre popcorn, drizzled in a hot perfume of silky melted butter. My mind even drifted to the perfect fatty chunk found in every can of Heinz Pork and Beans. Kiley was always the quickest to fish the fat out of the pot with the same laser focus she used while playing Operation. I never dreamed that pieces of wobbly pork fat would become my future jungle fantasy.

In the jungle, conversation always drifted to food, due to our lack of it. The pigs and chickens from the local village broke into our inventory, robbing us blind of everything but the canned mackerel, a diminishing bucket of peanut butter and some carrots. Our cookie stash had been contaminated by a leaking container of lantern kerosene, but in the end, we took the risk and ate them anyway, despite the toxic, metallic aftertaste and fumy breath.

We sat in tight circles under the palm frond roof of our hut, outdoing each other with cravings for sprinkle donuts and sweet and sour glazed meatballs. The Australian volunteers in our group were all desperate for slices of bread smeared with yeasty Vegemite. They spoke of Tim Tams (a malted chocolate layer biscuit) and jaffles (two pieces of bread, pressed and toasted with fillings like mac n' cheese, baked beans or ham and eggs, best enjoyed while camping) and patriotic Anzac biscuits (chewy oatmeal and golden syrup cookies). They rhymed off a wish list of several items that the majority of the Canadian and Costa Rican contingent hadn't heard of, but were all ears and taste buds to hear about.

When I moved to Toronto in 2002 (freed of the jungle worms I returned home with), a tempting world of international kitchens opened up before me. I was game for it all save for the canned brown rice beverage I bought in Koreatown on a soupy August afternoon. I was quite pleased with my discovery of Hodu Gwaja (walnut cakes) filled with a sweet red bean filling. The darling bite-size cakes are baked in moulds that resemble actual walnuts – so cute! What wasn't cute was the brown rice drink that (unbeknownst to me) had rice (as advertised) in the can. I shook it up, as the can directed, but didn't expect a mouthful of wet maggots. The maggots were actually rice, but even after I spat them out on the sidewalk along Bloor (in highly dramatic fashion) I still wasn't certain or reassured.

I worked my way through every mysterious menu option from tart Hungarian cold cherry soup to sushi fashioned out of panko-encrusted Kraft Dinner at Cardinal Rule on Roncesvalles Avenue. Thanks to *NOW* magazine's Food & Drink section, I had instant intel on where to find break-your-heart chicken and waffle donuts (Glory Hole Doughnuts), frothy peanut butter and jam lattes (Alligator Pear Café on Queen Street), traditional British mushy peas (Chippy's Fish & Chips in the Annex), Turkish lamb kebabs stuffed with neon pink pickled turnip and fat-strawed lychee bubble tea, heavy with Concord-grape coloured tapioca balls.

Michelle, my newish Northern friend from Nunavut (in love with a Toronto gal), frequently flew south with an Arctic swag bag of muskox or caribou, char jerky and real juniper berries that we'd chew on with gin.

My brother's bestie, David, shared the strange delight of Cantonese mooncake made with salted egg yolks and lotus seed paste. Dax took a hard pass in favour of another stiff ginger beer and vodka while I interrupted David throughout our weekly *Sex in the City* viewing get-togethers to ask about what other great mooncake-type things he might have up his Chinese sleeve.

My co-worker at the Fairmont Royal York Hotel spa introduced my brother and me to Byzantium on Church Street and the bar's signature potent fifteen-dollar three-ounce lychee martinis. How had I lived without lychee for so long? The apricot-like flesh absorbs alcohol like a flavour sponge.

I was lucky to live just blocks from Dax in The Village. We started shaking our own lychee martinis on Dax's panoramic balcony. I'm not sure whether the vertigo stemmed from being on the twenty-eighth floor or the stiff martinis he mixed us.

We met most weekends at Jet Fuel on Parliament Street for pint glasses of lethal double-shot mochaccinos. Like me, Dax was all legs and hated giving money over to public transit when we could walk. So, we walked. We went to Black Camel for slow-smoked pulled pork and rapini sandwiches wolfed back with bitter Brio chinotto sodas in the nearby park. Sometimes we'd poke around Kensington market, laughing at our exotic Jamaican beef patty in a coco bun decision. It was exactly that: a patty in a bun. Why would anyone want that when the patty was already wrapped in pastry?

We tried doughy corny Colombian arepas that we lost most of as we walked down Brunswick. A similar experience was had with banh mi subs as we left an accidental trail of daikon radish, cilantro and pork belly all the way to Dundas as we left Banh Mi Boys on Queen. The jerk oxtail from Mr. Jerk on Wellesley Street left us both wide-eyed from heat that was akin to a dynamite blast in our mouths.

Dax was an automatic yes to any food and drink show, CHIN picnic (a multicultural event sponsored by CHIN radio with international food and entertainment), or Greektown Taste of the Danforth celebration. The annual feverish Danforth street party results in more beer on you than in you.

We'd graze our way through sheep's milk cheese that tasted like sour socks, reviving our pinched taste buds with a sticky toffee-studded cheese from England. We ate dripping sugar waffle cones stuffed with sweet shredded pulled pork and tangy threads of coleslaw. Dax was my go-to wingman for beer festivals and champagne-tasting classes. "Do you taste wet cement? Granite countertop?" Yes! Cheers! We laughed at the pretentiousness of it all, but glugged back the offerings in a professional, studious manner.

After eating a small bite out of Toronto, I found myself on the other side of the world (circa 2008), ordering fried grasshoppers and a 750ml bottle of Nile beer at the Entebbe night market in Uganda.

That's right, Alan and Billy. Get a load of that! There was no handshake on a fifty-dollar bet or promise of a minibike at the end (though I did take a motorbike taxi to the market). My ten-year-old self would never believe that twenty-five years later, I'd be voluntarily eating fried grasshoppers without any ketchup or horseradish. Not even a squeeze of lemon or Alsatian sour cream sauce to disguise it.

Seasoned with a smoky, salty spice not unlike Kentucky Fried Chicken's eleven secret herbs and spices, fried grasshoppers, blindfolded, have a taste and crunch identical to chicken wing skin. Nan Torti would have had no part of this, KFC-likeness or not. She died a month after I arrived in Uganda at age eighty-four. Every time I had grasshoppers at the market, I could see Nan's drawn-on eyebrows comically arching in a mix of disgust and fear. "You'll die of hydrophobia!" If the worms didn't get me, it would be a fear of water, according to Nan. Somebody had obviously instilled this irrational phobia in her and it was her duty to let me know that everything from sharing ice cream cones with Xanadu to licking my fingers after a carnival ride induced it. Fried grasshoppers in Uganda would definitely be a shoo-in.

So, how do you eat fried grasshoppers? Easy. They're seasonal, so do your research. Next: find a roaming vendor with a five-litre pail of the fried de-winged and de-legged hoppers. They will be served in a folded piece of newspaper or some child's old math homework with a grin. Order a beer and keep an eye on the sly market cats who love fried grasshoppers seemingly more than mice.

If your grasshoppers are a day old, you can reheat them in the microwave to revive the intense flavour profile. I learned this trick from Ruth, the jolly housekeeper at the Jane Goodall Institute where I stayed in Entebbe. The kitchen reeked of hot insects for most of the day, but Ruth and the cats, Juwa and Pops, were quite pleased with the reheat, licking their fingers and whiskers respectively.

That's how you eat fried grasshoppers.

Adulterated

My calling has always been more dinner bell than "Hey, maybe I should become a chef!" I don't suit white (it washes me right out) and don't fare well in window-less places. One distracted nick with a knife and I battle to forgive myself for days for my sloppy inattention to something as basic as onion mincing.

I guess I am a food voyeur/culinary evangelist/interloper of sorts. A self-appointed junk food historian with credentials that include a lot of crumpled candy wrappers and diary entries about KFC. The briny shrimp bundled in bacon in the Bahamas was the kick-starter. I've been fascinated by the union of food and its universal bond ever since.

When communication fails, food speaks to us and for us. We look to fortune cookies for luck and epiphanies. We disguise chocolate truffles as an "I love you" and a dozen homemade chocolate chip cookies as a tail-between-the-legs "I'm sorry." We celebrate, mourn, marry and fall ill with food following us like a shadow. A remembered taste can transport us back to a time and place that no longer exists. A fried smelt remains dormant in my taste buds and olfactory until the *BOOM!* trigger of nostalgia.

Our five basic tastes (salty, sweet, sour, bitter and umami) lie in wait in our gustatory receptor cells. Take a bite of a baked pretzel, glossy with butter and sea salt, and your brain sends a text message to the insular cortex (also identified as the gustatory cortex) which makes us aware of the perception of taste. Or distaste.

Fire up the twelve million smell receptors in your nose and nasal cavity and one big whiff sends electrical signals to your brain's olfactory bulb for processing. The olfactory system and insular cortex are hot-wired to the amygdala, an area in the brain designed for emotional learning. The olfactory nerve is similar to the hippocampus, the campus where the brain downloads memories. Damage to this area of the brain impacts both memory and the ability to smell.

It's a wallop of nerdy science, but there's crunchy proof behind the mystical experience of the time machine ride that still-warm-from-the-oven apple crumble permits. The combination of ginger, nutmeg, cinnamon, buttery oats and soft apples grabs your hand and runs across the forest of fallen pine needles to Aunt Teresa's cottage on Clear Lake or the roadside stand you randomly stopped at in the Annapolis Valley, Nova Scotia, ten years ago.

Fond food memories, often attached to people and places, are no different than the soundtracks that resonate in our lives. I am bone-deep Cyndi Lauper, Boy George, Eurythmics, Pat Benatar, Tina Turner and a little bit Kenny Rogers. I am Sinead O'Connor, Jane Siberry, Belinda Carlisle and okay, okay, Vanilla Ice.

I'm a product of my time and it's revealed in song just as much as it is in my affection for frosted Pop-Tarts and pigs in a blanket. I am Hickory Sticks and cherry Kool-Aid. When I snoop in the shopping carts at our local Food-land I wonder – where did that come from? Obviously, it came from a shelf in the store, but I am curious about the who and when behind the chosen items. Like, what are you going to do with that fennel? Who introduced you to a turban squash? Why are you buying green pep-pers when red, yellow and orange taste so much better? Or sometimes I can't help but frown and think: how many people are you feeding?

I see carts void of our staples: avocadoes, tortilla wraps, naan, panko, sweet potatoes, cilantro, Patak's spicy butter chicken cooking sauce, grape tomatoes, chocolate soy milk, vanilla yogurt, White Fox aged white Leicester, some Gypsy salami, spinach, Harvest Cheddar Sun Chips and I almost throw the brakes. "What could you possibly be eating if you're not buying these things?"

I remind myself that we are all products of our past or complete reinventions of ourselves because of it. Insert Keto or Paleo diets here. I smile to see that Pop-Tarts and Kellogg's Frosted Mini-Wheats are still strong in circulation. I'm equally amazed to see white Dempster's Wonder Bread flying off the shelves in stiff competition with in-house bakery loaves of sourdough, focaccia peppered with kalamata olives and rosemary.

I think nine out of ten born in the '70s would agree that the very best grilled cheese sandwiches (or a "cheese grilled," in a nod to my dad) deserve white Wonder Bread.

But we've all grown up, haven't we? We've discovered Pad Thai, vindaloo, kimchi and California rolls. We roll with kombucha and Korean short ribs and Portuguese custard tarts. Even my mom buys couscous.

These curiously filled Foodland shopping carts make me think of *Welcome to Pine Point*. The 2011 interactive web documentary by Michael Simons and Paul Shoebridge, the former creative directors of *Adbusters* magazine, was as familiar as Tiffany's "I Think We're Alone Now" with a warm Tab on a summer's eve. The doc is an ode to a hometown where no one grew old or moved away. The documentary is a hybrid art book, film mashed up with a family photo album. It makes sense of this very book.

We all have our own Pine Point and era. For me, it was exactly what Simons and Shoebridge condensed into one paragraph: "It was maybe the last truly iconic era. The last time we more or less went through the motions of change together, everyone excited by the same things, at the same time."

The film illuminates the juxtaposition of sadness and gratitude in knowing that "It seems so much harder to be collectively surprised, exhilarated."

Back then we had anticipation, patiently waiting for the summer blockbusters to come to the local Cineplex. We counted the days until the carnival arrived at the Civic Centre or the Paris Fall Fair opened so we could finally get a corn dog striped with mustard. With movies on demand and corn dogs on demand (available in the freezer section of your nearest grocer), the exhilaration is gone. There's nothing to anticipate now.

Then, we held our breath for the overly anticipated McDonald's pizza debut in 1989. Crystal Pepsi blew our soda pop minds in 1992 with its cool new clear look and full-on Pepsi taste.

Everyone, I mean everyone, watched the same things, just like the Pine Point guys said. We were excited by the exact same things: *Family Ties*, *Growing Pains*, *Who's the Boss?*, *The Golden Girls*. Our parents watched the same stuff as our friends' parents: *Magnum P.I.*, *Hill Street Blues*, *Dynasty*, *The Young and the Restless*. There were only so many options – especially if you didn't have cable or satellite TV.

In the '80s and '90s, we were a collective, unstoppable force in squeaky white Tretorns, neon bangles, acid-washed jeans, Swatches and

Beaver Canoe sweatshirts. We ate McCain's oven fries and Taco Bell tacos. Birthdays could be celebrated at Mother's Pizza, Pizza Chief or Ponderosa. It was one or the other. Or, in this case, the other.

We didn't have Uber Eats or Foodora. We didn't have kimchi or banh mi or protein bars. There were no deep-fried pickles or cutesy bison sliders or baked buffalo cauliflower wings. The only avocado in Mount Pleasant was the colour of our fridge.

Perhaps this has all led me here, kinda surprised and exhilarated, craving both *Eurythmics Greatest Hits* and, oddly, some battered Chicken McNuggets with sweet 'n' sour sauce.

Our Own Private Island

Like most households, our kitchen is the hub of everything. The island serves as the drafting table for plotting trip itineraries abroad. It's where the daily news is read, emails are fired off and cups of coffee are nursed. It's a birdwatching blind as the back of our house is entirely windows that open to the tall stands of cedars and tamarack that surround us. The warblers cruise through the greenery like neon lightning bolts while the presence of overhead crows and gulls is revealed in silent shadows. Binoculars sit at the ready, just as they did in Nan Chapin's kitchen. We keep them in an oval galvanized metal bucket with bird guides and rolled Turkish blankets by the French doors, next to the orange cannon of a telescope that we negotiated over with the former house owners.

This private island of ours is one that Kim rejigged with sure hands and ergonomic considerations. It's four feet wide and ten feet long, which means four people could pull up a barstool and comfortably read *The Globe and Mail*. The barstools don't score well on ergonomics but they are cool and industrial-sleek. They suit our decision to incorporate corrugated steel onto the face of the island and shiplap on the ends. The existing body of the island was previously a two-tiered design with a cat barf-coloured laminate. The barstools that came with the house sale were definitely more comfortable but you couldn't tuck your legs under the countertop. After attempting to sit side saddle the first morning after we moved in, the island became the first mutual item on the chopping block. That is, after we painted every hickory cabinet and surface – which was endless. Two coats and three gallons of Behr Ultra Pure White (and just as much beer) later, the kitchen cabinets, bill paying station, butler's pantry cabinetry and shelving, built-in shelving in the open-concept living room and the primary bath vanity were sufficiently whitewashed.

The glass doors on the kitchen cabinets were permanently removed in favour of open shelving. The downlighting inside the cabinets became uplighting instead. The lower recessed panel cabinet doors with silver bin pulls, now white, provided just the aesthetic upgrade we wanted.

As Estée Lauder model Carolyn Murphy smartly said, "There is nothing white paint can't cure." We cured the mint chocolate chip green walls with more gallons of Behr Ultra Pure White, confident in our decision to create a neutral interior that pulled the outside in.

We ordered soapstone-look laminate countertops and boxes of polished charcoal grey ceramic subway tile. Kim patiently pieced the island together with the help of two friends well versed in renovations. They left their own renos to assist us with the promise of some play time on their kayaks over the Thanksgiving weekend.

Our private island was fitted with a drop-in brushed double-basin stainless steel sink and eighteen-inch commercial kitchen faucet with pull-down spray head. We switched out the dated, frosted pendant lights for clear, seeded glass and Edison bulbs. The bougie wine cooler was a chattel when we negotiated the house purchase – but we keep things casual by stocking it with beer, not wine.

This kitchen is minimalist and matchy – the polar opposite of both of our mothers' kitchens. Kim's mom had over one hundred glasses – I counted them all on their moving day. That number did not include the fifty-plus coffee mugs and ornate teacups, crystal sherry or shot glasses. My mom's collection (which I'm not allowed to count) is very miscellaneous with a fun assortment of thrift store finds, cocktail glasses that Dax has handed off in favour of a new style, dozens of champagne flutes and wine glasses that coordinate with the equally miscellaneous plate settings. Of all the options, everyone fights over the Earl's Albino Rhino pint glass I stole from a bar in Lethbridge, Alberta, when I was eighteen.

Here, we have only stemless wine glassware (and a few poached pint glasses, to be truthful). I'm down to my last Riedel, which is impressive after six moves. We have four La Rochere whiskey glasses that Kim pours red wine in. As if the glass knows the difference. Our prosecco glasses (the only line that we have eight of) have stems. Two of the champagne flutes are for celebrations only, which pulls them into action quite often. Kim bought them for me a decade ago so prior to every anniversary we ward off superstition and remind each other, "If the glass breaks, it doesn't mean anything!"

As my family will attest, I collect few things: books, passport stamps and beer glasses. Kim and I have pint and tulip beer glasses that we've managed to bring home, intact, from the Seychelles, Uganda, Iceland, Zanzibar, the Magdalen Islands and beyond.

We warn friends that they can't steal from us because with such limited inventory, we'll know immediately. Only six people can come for coffee. The two that see everyday rotation are white enamel-look mugs that resemble old-fashioned tin cups. There are two matching mugs with whimsical bird cages that my brother bought me in Newfoundland. The other two mugs are from my sister from Kicking Horse

Coffee in B.C., urging drinkers to "Wake up & kick ass." They are the only black items on our open shelves that house white everything.

Four white French Onion soup bowls, four square bowls, four round bowls, four shallow bowls, four large plates (round), four large plates (square) and four matching small rounds and squares. Those damned matching white plates that I carried two and a half kilometres from Kitchen Stuff Plus on Yonge Street to my apartment on Winchester Street in Toronto (pre-Kim). Too cheap to pay for a taxi, I stubbornly reasoned that I could carry the thirty-pound box home. Halfway, I wanted to collapse, surrender and cry my eyes out. I was certain that just ten feet from my doorstep, my arms would give out and the box would drop to the sidewalk, precious plates shattered. (It was a happy ending.) I am deeply attached to these plates for the hardship endured.

Even with our merged kitchens of Paderno pots and Ikea 365+ dinnerware, Kim and I can rarely fill the dishwasher because we don't have enough dishes. I end up picking out my favourite coffee mug and handwashing it, unable to wait for the fill three days later, defeating the purpose of a dishwasher's convenience.

Here, everything must have purpose. Any kitchen item that is not used is put on probation. When I start eyeballing Kim's big Corelle stoneware casserole dish, she quickly fishes out the only recipe that calls for that dish – her mom's "Easy Chicken" with liquid gravy browner, curry, Worcestershire, chicken bouillon, rosemary, thyme and parsley.

We have three bamboo cutting boards and just as many charcuterie boards, one of them sanded as smooth as pudding by Kim from the black walnut she built our former kitchen table out of.

We have a hand blender that my mom insisted we needed for a proper kitchen but in eight years, we've never found a purpose for it. Dax supplied us with a SodaStream, because it's integral to his kitchen. Each time my sister visits she asks if I am using "her" salad tongs – the silver pair with engraved fish on the handles that she bought in Nepal, for me. "I'll take them back if you're not." She knows about my probationary ways.

Open any of our drawers – we won't cringe. I can rattle off the precise inventory: a whale and owl bottle opener, a box of matches from Cigar Landing on Pier 17 in New York. A set of Laguoile knives. Kim's mother's measuring spoons. A solar flashlight. The little pâté knife we pocketed from Bar Volo. A Williams-Sonoma spatula and a miniature grater that I love to use for non-miniature blocks of cheese, even though it's intended for garlic cloves.

We keep a minimal amount of Tupperware, all of it matching. I start breathing heavy in the homes of friends upon accidentally opening a drawer that reveals a Tupperware cache that has extended to include empty yogurt and sour cream containers.

We have few kitchen rules, but crappy pans gotta go. If scrambled eggs start sticking on a frying pan, it's time to invest in a new T-fal or Rock. Pronto. After a month of using thirty shitty frying pans in hostels across Spain, Kim and I have zilch frying pan patience left.

During an extended visit at Christmas, Kiley asked why we didn't have any big spoons. I removed them from the cutlery drawer long ago because they were too big to politely eat anything with. They were quickly discontinued after I suffered near lockjaw from trying to accommodate both the spoon and Life cereal in my mouth. During the same visit/inspection, as Dax ran an index finger over our collection of cookbooks, he asked, "Have you used any of these?"

No. But I loved reading them. The cookbooks are for display purposes only (with apologies to chefs Jamie Oliver, Sean Brock, Lynn Crawford and Alice B. Toklas). The recipes we do use or fantasize about using are clipped together according to broad categories like Burgers + Pizza, Cocktails and Sweets, tucked neatly in a large Ziploc bag. Sweets! In my imagined life as an imaginary baker I will make Sweet Potato Cornmeal Biscuits, Chocolate Avocado Pudding, Dark Chocolate Beet Brownies, Spiced Squash and Carrot Loaf, No Knead Rosemary Garlic Bread and then, Rosemary Butter Cookies.

We have our staples as couples do and it's usually Kim who experiences a flavour flatline and desire to try a new recipe. A typical week includes butter chicken pizza, hickory-smoked pork and pineapple quesadillas, panko tilapia tacos with mango salsa, homemade chicken tortilla soup and greens piled high with avocado, corn, grape tomatoes and fried tortilla strips. Kim and I operate a gastropub of sorts. I'm not big on leftovers, which means anything we make is also minimal – not a stockpile-the-freezer event of multiple chilis and soups.

We live without all the gadgety things: Ninjas, Instant Pots, Kitchen Aids and rice cookers. We have a panini press and Cuisinart coffee maker that make everything we really, truly need.

Our kitchen is us. It would be inadequate for many. The adjacent acacia dining room table comfortably seats six on sand-coloured roll-top tufted upholstered side chairs but everyone gathers on the non-ergonomic stools around the island. We mix square and round plates to accommodate six but if there are four, perfect! Matching plates all around. We apologize for our two-slice toaster and the slow service. For three hundred and sixty days of the year, it's our domain, so the apology is half-hearted.

No, we don't have a gravy boat, teapot, roasting pan or flour. Or baking soda. We don't have a pie plate. Will a baking sheet do? We have one of those for making sweet potato fries, not cookies, of course.

You won't find a timer, an apron, cake slicer, ice cream scoop, loose tea ball, rolling pin, pressure cooker, salad spinner, mortar and pestle, Dutch oven, parchment paper, cooling racks, food processor, spiralizer, scale or coffee grinder. Oh – and if you use the colander, you'll definitely lose all the orzo down the drain.

What we do have is each other and a similar palate. While I'm more regimented in "food flow" and abide by a set of strict rules, Kim is admirably as versatile as a turkey vulture. On the flip side, I am not capable (or willing) to drink a beer after a bowl of cereal or to follow up butter chicken on rice with hot chocolate and marshmallows.

Ask anyone and they will tell you that Kim eats like the house is on fire. I eat like a bear, falling in and out of hibernation mode. I eat slowly and thoughtfully – if I have a newspaper in front of me, my bowl of Life will be soggy in no time. I have to reheat my coffee ten times before I finish a mug. Kim downs hers like it's a chugging contest. She continues to be amazed at how long I can stretch a meal. Invite my brother for dinner and serve us fries and it's an all-night affair.

Kim blames thirty-two years of shiftwork for her competition-style eating. She can drain a beer like she's getting rid of incriminating evidence. I'd get hiccups drinking at half her speed. Seated side by side, it's a showcase of savour versus survival.

In the grocery store aisles, Kim takes an efficient, targeted route. I get sidetracked by things I'm not even interested in purchasing: lemon curd in a jar, Barilla Ready Pasta (the pre-cooked pasta only requires a sixty-second reheat in the microwave) or chicken hearts in the deli. It doesn't take long for Kim to realize that I've lost focus in the international aisle and am most likely examining a can of Jamaican ackee.

We are so perfect for each other, slowing and hurrying each other in just the right increments. Kim is my equilibrium, bringing me necessary practicality and grounding. Travelling, she is my ideal partner with her willingness to be experimental, but also realistic. She has infinite patience for my stubborn quests.

Sure, she'll try blood sausage at a night market in the Seychelles or roadside grilled chicken after assessing the sanitation of the oil barrel BBQ conversion. But she's not afraid to give me a hard no to restaurants with a sawdust floor and bedsheets serving as walls (as suggested in Alexandria, Egypt).

Kim will traipse with me, wherever we are in the world, menu to menu, with a smile. She never travels with her reading glasses, so I become the default audio book, reading off the menu highlights. To which Kim will respond, "Do you really want cow foot soup?" Maybe. And we press on because I want to try lionfish before we leave Curaçao.

She walked five kilometres in blinding snow and bitter January gales to find a burger joint that I had read about. At the breaking (hypothermic) point, we found Chez Victor and with frozen faces unable to form words, we managed pints of Boreale Noire Stout and Griffon Rousse. I had a *cerf* (venison) burger with pears braised in red wine. Kim ordered *le sanglier* (wild boar) burger with brandied portobellos and rosemary-maple mayo and agreed, it was worth the polar expedition. It's simply what we do. Or, more often, what I convince Kim to do.

Kim is always game to track down the peanut butter and jam burgers or peppercorn-infused beer I've researched and read reviews about or drive in the opposite direction for a lasagna-stuffed grilled cheese. Even after walking nearly thirty kilometres along the Camino de Santiago earlier in the day, Kim still followed me in circles around León, Spain, as I was desperate to find the bar that had old farm implements and taxidermy on display. When we couldn't find it, we walked in a new direction, for another two kilometres, trying to locate the "Hell-Mex, psychobilly bar." It was closed on Mondays so I can't even tell you what Hell-Mex or psychobilly means.

Wherever we are, I'm sure to sniff out the strangest option and local fermentation. Kim is there, at my side, ready to clink glasses of banana gin, potato gin, potato vodka or cashew wine. From mind-erasing hash muffins in Amsterdam to wild boar burgers in Quebec City, I've found my unstoppable sidekick. Left to her own devices, Kim would be happy with a parking lot hot dog from a vendor outside of the Home Depot. At the same time, Kim knows that I would be much happier with a Nashville fried chicken sandwich, a pint of a local IPA and a little ambience. And sometimes we eat parking lot hot dogs, because that's what love means.

I need Kim in my life to remind me of all my past barfs and shats in the most loving way. The dodgy sugarcane juice in Cairo (that left both of us with hot diarrhea in advance of a hot air balloon ride). *Remember the homemade coconut cookies and "river juice" from the guy that hopped on the public bus in Placencia, Belize?* Then there's the ghost pepper hot sauce I singed my lower lip on after dousing my slice of fried egg pizza with the liquid lava in Samana, Dominican Republic. The inside of my lip still bubbles up with a bitchy blister with exposure to the lowest pepper on the Scoville scale (pepperoncini).

My amygdala will only respond to Kim's barbecued beer can chicken, seasoned with garlic, dill, cracked pepper and steamed inside out with pilsner. Her beef burritos fragrant with cumin. Kim's roasted potatoes freckled with paprika and gobs of butter. Her moist turkey burgers with the restaurant-like grill marks on a brioche bun. Her hot cocoa stirred with a pour of Nicaraguan rum. Even a simple slice of sourdough toast that she has carefully smeared with the scantest amount of peanut butter and jam (the only way I like it), slid in my direction as I write, says I love you. In return, I smother her toast with an inch of Kraft peanut butter (not my all-natural Adams) and spread enough strawberry jam to make her breakfast look like a murder scene (the only way Kim likes it). It says I love you too, *but please don't eat that toast in front of the laptop.*

We are opposites in so many ways, but we match perfectly where it matters most. Kim has filled my hungry gap. She is everything I had been craving.

The Old Kitchen Sink

Last summer, after a regenerative week camping at Long Point Provincial Park, my wife and I tacked a few nights on to our getaway to spend time with friends on Splatt's Bay in Dunnville. It was a five-hour, hamstring-curling drive back to our home on the Northern Bruce Peninsula.

As Kim made the turn due north from the shores of Lake Erie towards Lake Huron I said, "Let's cut through Six Nations and then Mount Pleasant." Our route back to Lion's Head was a spaghetti noodle mess of side roads anyway. We could drive right past my childhood house if we detoured a little.

Picking at our emergency peanut butter Clif bars because we were unable to decide on or find a place to eat along the way, I almost didn't recognize the T-intersection at Pleasant Ridge Road. "Here! Turn left!"

Kim cranked the Jeep wheel towards Arthur Road and I pointed out the highlights (not for the first time) without taking a breath. "There's the manure tank that Dax pulled my younger cousin out of when he went for an accidental swim." I showed her the tractor shed which was the ultimate hide-and-seek hiding spot – especially if you had time to wedge yourself into the combine. "Look, that's the sign my grandfather hammered up nearly two decades ago warning drivers to watch for dogs playing with mice in the ditches." To the left, my grandparents' house! It's where I found my first star-nosed mole in the earth when Grandpa was digging out the foundation for the house. "There's the pond where we'd snag sunfish and catfish with any kind of bait – even mini marshmallows." The memories rushed in all at once.

"Slow down ... that was Grandma's house. The tobacco kilns. Look at the walnut trees, still!" I prepared for the bump in the road but the train tracks no longer existed; they had been pulled up a decade ago for a proposed rail trail. Our red brick ranch seemed so nestled in the trees. I couldn't believe how the trees had grown – without me.

"Do you want me to stop?" Kim asked. I was already rooting around for our camera.

"Yes, please. Just for a minute so I can get a pic to send to Kiley and Dax."

I pushed my bare feet back into my flip-flops and crossed the road to take a better picture from the end of the driveway, zooming in on the house. The cedars had been pulled out and the front door looked different but it was still very much our house. The stately paper bark birch that stood in front of my old bedroom window was long gone and the mature pine forest had thinned behind the house too.

Snap. Snap. I watched through my camera lens as the front door swung open.

"Why the f*** are you taking pictures of my house?"

Shaken but not stirred I hollered back, "I used to live here."

The homeowner took a step forward. "You're Larry and Sandy's kid?"

"Yeah."

His face warmed and gave way to a smile. "I'm Ken. Do you wanna come in and take a look around?"

I didn't know if I wanted to. Walking through Grandma's house years before was different. I wasn't as attached. I wasn't expecting an offer or someone to open the door at all but felt the pull to check it out. Kim shrugged and nodded, overhearing the invite. She was content to sit and wait.

As soon as I crossed the threshold, I felt the sparkly and surreal suspension of time in a house that was no longer mine. The iconic brick arches in the entryway were the only remnants of my youth. The shag carpet and the living room's lethal gold wheat sheath table (that we all nearly lost an eyeball to) remained only in the attic of my mind. The louvred closet doors shiny with a layer of orange oil wood polish, gone. The lemon meringue pie plaster ceiling had been replaced in favour of drywall and recessed lights. I looked down half-expecting to see Xanadu tucked under the highboy where he'd curl up like a shrimp to sleep.

I could see clean into the kitchen from where I stood. Puzzled, I realized that the brick wall that separated the living room and kitchen was totally gone – the ol' ranch had been given a proper open concept treatment.

"Come in, take a look around, really." Ken apologized for his initial reaction and swearing. "We get a lot of weirdos around here."

My parents sold the house in the fall of 2000 and I had moved out six years before that after my jungle foray. What a time warp! I pointed out the linen closet where I used · to stuff Dax, groaning, "G-R-E-M-L-I-N-S" in the creepiest voice possible, scratching the door with my nails to totally freak him out. How did he ever fit in there? The house felt compressed. Maybe I was simply taller?

Ken's wife joined in on the tour with a bubbly self-introduction. I blabbed about how Dax and I both had waterbeds and she was amazed that anything but a waterbed fit in the tiny bedrooms. "Oh, and we found your forest mural under the barnboard. Lovely," she laughed. The mural was commonly associated with dentist offices in the '80s, but I was desperate for the wall-to-wall, floor-to-ceiling woods in my bedroom. My teen bedroom had been stripped, deforested. A clear-cut of time.

"Do you like beer?" Ken asked.

I thought he was offering me a beer for a proper house tour – it was noon after all. He hurried to what used to be our laundry room and returned with four beers and a branded lager glass. His wife filled in the blanks for me. "We own Brewer's Blackbird Kitchen + Brewery in Ancaster. This is our beer."

Blackbirds. How perfect. I could hear them in an instant. The red-winged blackbirds peppered the skies and bent cattails to the ground around the pond with their numbers each spring. As dusk shadowed the countryside, the deep chorus of peepers replaced the melody of the blackbirds, both celebrating the return of warmer days.

I was pulled around the house and advised of the changes, in case I didn't remember. "Oh, look, a walking stick!" Ken's wife kneeled beside the window screen in the living room where the prehistoric-looking insect peered in. "We love being so immersed in nature here." The couple gushed about turtles coming up from the pond to nest in the front flowerbeds. I nodded along, sharing my David Attenborough-inspired years, tracking the painted and snapper turtles by marking their shells with my mom's nail polish.

Memories ping-ponged from all angles. My great-grandfather used to catch turtles from the same pond and sell them to Chinese restaurants in the city. Rabbits and squirrels too. I left that part out.

I took a few pictures for posterity but my lifetime lived at RR#2 remains an unchangeable, treasured album of its own. Like the clock that stopped in our kitchen; the hands that never moved again. My time stood still. My childhood home is now a place of walking sticks, starry dreams and blackbirds for somebody else.

The sliding doors were still in the same place but they now opened to an expansive deck and hot tub. The appliances had all been updated and rearranged for flow. It made sense but the coziness (okay, cramped-ness) was gone. A ginger cat yawned, stretched and approached me for a scratch. I wonder if she sensed the legendary cats before her. I wonder if she had an automatic feeder like Drakkar.

I thanked Ken profusely and walked back to the Jeep holding up the four-pack of beer like a trophy when I caught Kim's attention. There was still a whiff of heady pig manure in the air. It was the kind of hazy, halcyon August afternoon when my mom would declare it was too hot to cook on the stove. The hibachi would appear and with a healthy squirt of accelerant, we'd impatiently wait for the charcoal briquettes to blister and glow.

We never had a propane or electric barbecue – it was always the non-ergonomic hibachi on the garage floor. What should have been a six-minute steak took sixty minutes start to finish with the old-school grill.

Back in the Jeep with Kim's fingers laced in mine, golden corn and rye fields whisking by, I suddenly yearned for well-charred meat swimming in HP sauce. Some of my mom's mayo-heavy potato salad studded with radish, celery and gherkins. And paprika. Just a sprinkle. And a warm Coca-Cola. The purr of tractors in the fields. The blackbirds, the peepers. The innocence.

I felt the absence of Nan Chapin, her home now merely a house again too. As the cobwebs of dementia made her solitary rural life dangerous, the family decided to move her into the "memory wing" of a long-term care facility on the edge of the city in Brantford. Nan had lived on Arthur Road her entire life. She was a fixture, just like the kilns and silos. Her farm and acreage have been condensed to a simple furnished room with a single window to the world beyond. A framed aerial photo of the Chapin farm taken decades before hangs on a wall, a mere slice of time when the geese gathered by the hundreds around her pond and the corn stretched so tall towards autumn, she couldn't see the approach of my grandfather's truck near harvest.

I wonder if Nan could see us in that aerial shot, goofing around, balancing on the train tracks, pretending to be Olympian gymnasts, distracted from our asparagus picking task? Would she remember how to make her buttery white sauce for asparagus on toast? Could she see her intricately set table at Christmas, with nearly thirty chairs and plates assembled around makeshift tables of sawhorses and plywood? The serving trays filled with gherkins and pickled onions? The Schwartz Mustard card suit glasses filled to the brim with thick glugs of Heinz tomato juice? What about her famous green fluff? Would Nan remember how to make that if all the ingredients were placed before her? She never referred to a recipe card, ever.

How could everything familiar become so foreign? How does the back of your own hand seemingly belong to a stranger one day? How can an aerial shot of your old farm transform into nothing but a nice picture, like something you'd see in a free calendar from the bank?

How can the brain forget what it loved most? I suppose that's the saving grace of dementia. Eventually you forget that you no longer remember.

But still. Would the smell of Nan's dim root cellar, musty and earthen with root veg in bushel baskets and dusty potato sacks pull her back? If she heard the purple martin's song, would she recall the bird clock that hung in her kitchen above the microwave? Would she suddenly remark, "Is it seven o'clock already?" Or, when she heard the purple martin's loud burst of song at dawn, just before night splits into day, would she fall into the embrace of her own childhood, so similar to mine with the smell of sun-bleached corn and tobacco curing in the kilns across the road?

Would she see a robin tugging on a lazy spring worm and think aloud, with a knee slap and uninhibited laugh, "How was it that you were supposed to eat fried worms anyway?"

Corn fields. Candy corn.

Fields of hay. Chocolate haystacks.

Green grass. Green fluff.

Tobacco. Popeye cigarettes.

Purple martins. Purple Kool-Aid.

We remember and then we forget.

And then we don't remember what we've forgotten.

Doggy Bag

Nightcap

I was unnaturally sad when the headlines on June 8, 2018, revealed that Anthony Bourdain had committed suicide at age sixty-one while on location in France, filming an episode for CNN's *Parts Unknown*. He sits in my head whenever I write about food, especially burgers. He once said, "Writing a blog about burgers is like keeping a diary while having sex." I was red-faced guilty on all accounts.

Before I had a face to associate with the name, I knew Bourdain for his book *Kitchen Confidential: Adventures in the Culinary Underbelly*, published in 2000. Then came the Food Network debut of *A Cook's Tour*, the Travel Channel's *Anthony Bourdain: No Reservations*, *The Layover* and *Anthony Bourdain: Parts Unknown*.

He was my dream boyfriend, replacing my teen crush on the rakish and aloof River Phoenix, who died of a drug overdose in 1993. The jacket cover of Bourdain's *A Cook's Tour: In Search of a Perfect Meal* is an image I would still thumbtack above my bed. Tony stands jauntily in his denim and camouflage muscle shirt, a messenger bag slung over his shoulder. There's a slight smirk, a pierced ear and just the beginnings of his affection for tattoos from around the world. His arms are nearly bare of ink. He's all curiosity and questions.

Bourdain had already latched onto what elevated simple dishes like borscht or tiger prawns. It was the weathered faces and practiced hands behind them. It was decades of survival, family bloodlines, political upset, turbulent history and tradition steeped into a dish. It was never about the food; it was the people behind it and the knowledge embedded in their DNA.

I felt like we had spent so much time together. I had sat next to and across from Anthony Bourdain on planes and two-tops from Ho Chi Minh City to Tehran. When Kim and I were in Cartagena, Colombia, in 2015, we made a drowsy jetlagged beeline to La Cevicheria on Calle Stuart because Anthony said we should. My TripAdvisor review rings so true today that I can hear and feel the chaos of the street, the rush of cold beer sliding down our parched throats. We split a lime-licked octopus-squid-snapper-shrimp-mango ceviche and knew immediately that it would be the best thing we'd eat in Cartagena.

In September 2019, in downtown St. John's, Newfoundland, we were guided by Bourdain's ghost to a former cigar bar called Christian's for an authentic "screech-in" ceremony complete with a sample of Newfoundland steak (bologna). Raising the almighty shot of rum, we recited the words as Bourdain did in October 2017: "Long may your jib draw." There's a pillar with his engraved name and a framed photo of his classic, charismatic mug.

We weren't the only ones to fall under the spell of the Bourdain effect. The province's tourism department showed a 207 percent spike in visits to the NewfoundlandLabrador.com website after his *Parts Unknown* episode. It rounded out our itinerary as we followed in Bourdain's iconic desert boot footsteps to the historic Mallard Cottage located in the beating heart of Quidi Vidi Village for cod cakes and the best veg hash I've ever had. Maybe it was knowing Bourdain had been there too, but the turnip, parsnip, carrot with a yolky egg and sharp cheese confirmed this guy was on to something.

Just as baseball fanatics fantasize about eating a hot dog in every stadium in the United States, I wondered if Kim and I should get real and follow Bourdain's blazed trail from São Paulo to Taipei. I'm sure someone has done it or is licking their lips and giving thanks somewhere along the way.

Naturally, CNN is desperate to find their next Bourdain. It's impossible, of course. *Stanley Tucci: Searching for Italy*? Nah, Emmy Awards or not, I'll do my own Italy search without poker-face Tucci. The National Geographic series *Gordon Ramsey: Unchartered*? Nah, I don't want to go to Louisiana's Bayou or Hawaii's Hana Coast without Anthony. I'd be better convinced by the likes of British actress Joanna Lumley, who is as bubbly and refreshing as a flute of champagne. Or Chef Lynn Crawford. She's approachable, sophisticated and casual all at once. And that laugh! Contagious. But. Still. Anthony.

I've been ruined. By Anthony Bourdain. By my grandmothers who made me love the oddest and simplest things: fried smelts, fish eyes, green fluff, puffballs and sailboat sandwiches. And Cinnabons, of course. My mother has spoiled me rotten the most. No one can match her savoury cabbage rolls and decadent pecan pie. She has connected the generational divide with her oil-splattered recipe cards, confident hands and floured apron. I can't even buy a bag of flour or sugar.

Most importantly, my mother has taught me to be interested and forever curious, so there's that.

I will remain inspired, curious and steadfast, wet nose pointed in the air like a German Short-haired Pointer. With every passport stamp I will remember to stay hungry and to listen for the purple martins.

I will remember how to eat fried worms and grasshoppers.

Tasting Notes

A highlight reel of questionable things I've eaten, in no particular order.

Fermented shark, Bjarnarhofn Shark Museum, Dalvik, Iceland: One cube of Greenland shark (*hákarl*) on a toothpick is all Kim and I needed to get the gist. The overpowering ammonia smell from fermentation killed off any potential to really taste the shark. The aftertaste lingered long after. Too long after.

"Love Balls," The Nesbrud Bakery, Stykkisholmur, Iceland: This bakery is a wonderland with several varieties of twists and sugared rolls dunked in severe amounts of icing, and *astarpungar* ("love balls"). These dense doughnuts are the size of a squash ball and mildly tart with a hit of lemon and cardamom.

Reindeer burger, Kaffi Hornið, Hofn, Iceland:
This hip resto-cafe is housed inside an impressive
log cabin vibrating with locals watching
European football. Though the specialty in these
parts is langoustine, I had to do the reindeer
burger with red onion jam and a wham of blue
cheese. Kim chose the perky paprika soup to
warm her damp bones.

Deep-fried guinea pig, Quito, Ecuador: I barfed
for several days across the Galapagos Islands
after eating guinea pig but a finger of blame
could also be pointed to the two raw eggs I
had for breakfast, slugged back Rocky-style. I
shared the guinea pig with an affable Australian
who was keen on the local delicacy. It came to
the table intact, eyes, ears, teeth and all, heavily
battered and dusted with spices. I took the head
back to my hotel room for a photo because I'd
forgotten my camera. All night my stomach
churned, smelling only the deep-fried guinea pig
skull in my garbage can.

**Grilled piranha and fire ant hot sauce, some-
where along the Orinoco River, Venezuela:** It
was somewhat surreal dining on the river that inspired an Enya song, the famous "Orinoco Flow."
I didn't dream that I'd be eating piranha in Venezuela – or fishing for them. My hook came up
bare but the Toronto couple I shared a boat with
snagged a few and later that night we ate the
luscious fish with dots of electric hot sauce made
from the crushed bodies of fire ants.

Deep-fried Mars bar, at The Wee Chippie, Mission, BC: Submerged in the fryer, a Mars bar takes on a whole new flavour dimension.

Deep-fried Oreos, Edmonton Folk Festival, Edmonton, AB: I haven't had another Oreo since this untouchable 2012 event, fearful that I will mess with my limbic system and this precious memory.

Deep-fried crab-stuffed avocado at Landry's and "Armadillo Eggs" at T-bone Tom's Steakhouse, Kemah, Texas: On the eighth day, God made deep-fried jalapeño balls stuffed with pulled pork and called them something fancy: Armadillo Eggs. At Landry's Seafood House we uncovered the ball show-stopper: crab-stuffed avocado, fried and served with a heavy-duty chipotle ranch dip and fire-breather side salsa.

Sichuan numb & spicy pork dish, Wuhan, China: I learned too late how to say *"bu yao."* It means "I don't want it." The Sichuan numb and spicy pork dish skidded my no-holds-barred adventurous eating to a halt. My tongue tingled and then went into a terrifying numbed state for a very disturbing twenty minutes. This dish is like party drugs for your mouth – and the party takes too long to come to an end.

Caribou (the drink), Hôtel de Glace, Quebec: Served in a glass carved out of ice, Caribou is an authentic French-Canadian esophagus warmer. The boozy blend of red wine, whiskey and maple syrup works wonders in warding off the sub-zero temps of the hotel.

Quidi Vidi Iceberg Lager, Bonavista, Newfoundland: I was expecting a generic lager but the indigo blue-bottled beer does have a distinct taste which must be the 20,000-year-old icebergs it's brewed with. On a similar note, I had a DIY iceberg martini at the Jökulsárlón Lagoon. With a foraged chunk of the Breiðamerkurjökull Glacier and a glug of Reykjavík Vodka, it was a refreshing, historical sip.

Cod cheeks, Puffin Café, Elliston, Newfoundland: At first the cheeks are an agreeable bite, but after a few scallop-sized "cheeks" Kim and I were ready to surrender, overloaded by the richness of the dish, served with a wallop of creamy tartar and fried scrunchions (salt pork rinds and pork fat).

Fried grasshoppers, Tuesday night market, Entebbe, Uganda: Skeptics will be amazed by the addictive crunch. Grasshoppers are the perfect side to skewers of goat grilled over coals or a Ugandan "Rolex" (a chopped cabbage, tomato and onion omelette rolled inside a warm stoneground chapati flatbread). Order a Stoney Tangawizi too. The non-alcoholic ginger beer is so spicy you'll have a coughing fit through most of it.

Covered Bridge "Storm Chips," Charlottetown, Prince Edward Island: Maritimers know to stock up on these above all else in the event of an approaching hurricane. Stephanie Domet, a CBC Radio One host, is credited with coining the term. It was innocent enough – she was simply talking about her desire to stock up on some storm chips and dip after work. The hashtag #stormchips landed like a tsunami. New Brunswick's Covered Bridge brand sells official Storm Chips, designed for hurricanes, blizzards or any ol' storm-stayed day. The combo consists of their four best sellers: Smokin' Sweet BBQ, Homestyle Ketchup, Creamy Dill and Sea Salt & Vinegar. I found a bag at the tail end of summer at a P.E.I. gas station and Atlantic Canada is definitely taking all necessary precautions.

Termites, Caves Branch Archaeological Reserve, Belize: There's no better way to end a day of lazily cave tubing than a pick-me-up snack of live termites. Strangely, they taste exactly like scrambled eggs.

Cashew wine, Hopkins Village, Belize: It sounded so promising because cashews are so satisfying. As a wine, not so much. It was sickly sweet and weird. Was it rebranded, rebottled cough syrup?

Cow's tongue, Caplansky's Deli, Toronto: Growing up, there was always a great thrill to be found in the deli section of Calbecks grocery store. "Let's go poke the cow tongues!" Shrink-wrapped in cellophane on Styrofoam plates, the tongues were irresistible to kid fingers. Poke. Poke. Eating one was a similar situation. Poke. Poke. It was feathery and buttery. But eating something that is already found in your own mouth is extremely weird.

Jerk oxtail stew, Mr. Jerk, Toronto: Dax and I split an order that needed a fire hose as a side. Instead, it came with slaw, rice and peas and starchy plantain that did little to calm the fires within.

Escargot pizza, Il Fornello, Toronto: The brackish bites of chewy escargot merge amazingly well with a wood-fired pizza slathered with just a skim of tomato sauce and mozza.

Oyster juice stout, Dublin, Ireland: The memory is murky but it was definitely a stout and a shot of oyster juice to round out a tipsy bar crawl around the Temple Bar district.

Oolichan / Eulachon / Candlefish, Vancouver, BC: It's like eating fish in a melted lip balm sauce.

Daddy long legs spider, Brantford Collegiate Institute, Brantford, ON: Laura Toth bet me ten bucks that I wouldn't eat a spider, so I did, Billy Forrester *How to Eat Fried Worms*-style. I was grateful for the pizza slice financing that Laura provided that week.

Raw herring, on a yacht in Holland: Ken, the boat captain, grossed us out and then encouraged us to follow suit by swallowing slick lengths of raw herring. This was followed by a shot of Advocaat (an eggnog-like liqueur) which is not a recommended pairing with fish.

Space muffin, The Dolphins on Kerkstraat, Amsterdam: Kim and I planned to rent bikes to ride along the trails around Amsterdam Noord and believed that a space muffin would make for a cheap, portable picnic. Do not repeat. I repeat, DO NOT REPEAT. The muffin was really a cupcake weighted down by two inches of aqua blue icing with an equally neon signature gummy dolphin on top. Initially, Kim and I were upset that we had blown five euros on splitting a hash muffin that had no trippy effect. That is, until the muffin took effect and we lost the next eight hours to la la land.

Haggis, Burns Night, some forgotten Queen Street pub in Toronto: I loved it! It was fragrant and savoury. The sheep lungs, heart and liver give it a bad rap but the rest of the guts (oatmeal, cayenne and beef suet) marry well with a pint on a bitter January eve.

Civet shit coffee, Vancouver: It was all the rage and ten bucks for a slurp. It didn't change my life but it was one trend I didn't want to miss out on. The blend is courtesy of the Asian palm civet that eats coffee cherries and has a crap. Some entrepreneur thought, Hey, I bet the North Americans will pay ridiculous amounts to drink this Kopi luwak with a date square. They were dead right!

Caribou jerky via Nunavut: It's always good to have friends in high places and northern places too. My pal Michelle's former NU address allowed me to sample everything from Arctic char to muskox to caribou jerky.

Goat testicles, Lubumbashi, Congo: When in Rome, or, in this case, Lubumbashi … The testicles were served rather plainly as a gamey, ballsy entrée. They weren't terrible but I'm satisfied with the one-off.

Frog legs, Lubumbashi, Congo: I was wowed by so many meals in the Congo from frog legs to chocolate-plugged croissants from La Brioche to ham and banana pizza. Banana! The perfect alternative to pineapple in a pinch! These crispy, crunchy frog legs were my first and I'm a believer.

Crocodile pizza, The Dutchess, Fort Portal, Uganda: After a bumpy, lumpy five-hour sardine bus ride from Kampala, the outdoor space at The Dutchess is lively and arty. The menu offers croc ribs and smoked crocodile pizza. They also have precious Dutch gouda and brie for sale in their lobby. God bless the Dutch and their exports.

Dandelion latte, Oso Negro, Nelson, BC: It was hard to imagine what this might taste like. I didn't expect the likeness to chicken soup broth.

Chicha, Alto Cuen, Costa Rica: It's fermented corn hooch and it looks exactly like what you'd throw up after eating corn on the cob. It's vinegary, chunky and will make you spacey if you can get past the texture.

Fermented fig moonshine, Siwa Oasis, Egypt: Kim and I were convinced that we had shaken hands on the deal of the century on this one. For seven bucks we were handed a dusty recycled pop bottle of punky shine. It was so potent we eventually poured it down the sink of our hotel bathroom – and couldn't enter the room for an hour without our eyes watering.

Camel stew, Al Babenshal, Siwa Oasis, Egypt: Everything about this day and night was magical, lending well to the romance and exotica of it all. The camel stew was thick with sweet carrots, roasted potatoes, spicy plum tomatoes and tender camel that tastes like beef, not chicken. We sat on the rooftop of the thirteenth-century fortress and felt like royalty. In fact, royalty was dining directly beside us – the King of Siwa Oasis.

Roasted ant cotton candy, mealworm grilled cheese, chocolate-covered crickets, Cambridge Butterfly Conservatory, Cambridge, ON: I was lucky to have a job interview at the Conservatory during BugFEAST®, a highly-anticipated annual March Break event. Designed for the kiddos, I was privy to the buffet post-interview. There was also some fat maggoty type worm that burst in my mouth in a way that ruined my taste buds for the roasted ant cotton candy.

Fried egg potato chips, somewhere along the Camino de Santiago, Spain: Andrés Gourmet nailed the huevo frito flavour! Unfortunately, when you open the breakfast-in-a-chip-bag it smells exactly like a giant fart.

Susur Lee's cheeseburger spring rolls, Church Street, Pride Toronto: This fusion spring roll delivers a big bite of Americana into a crispy, golden Asian-inspired wrapper. Spring rolls are the perfect vehicle, really. Move over, brioche bun!

Pickled watermelon, somewhere: Who knew watermelon rinds could be pickled? I was so surprised I can't even remember where I tried them!

Pickled walnuts, Denny's House, Toronto: A Brit through and through, Denny always had a murky jar of them in her fridge. The walnuts are soft in texture and pickle-y, as advertised, steeped in brine the colour of strong tea.

Milkweed salad, Langdon Hall Country House Hotel & Spa, Blair, ON: Milkweed! The delicate young seed pods look like small, silvery sardines and were an unexpected salad addition. Executive Chef Jason Bangerter and the culinary team at Langdon Hall receive so many glowing reviews that the inn can be seen from outer space.

Absinthe at Gusto 101, Toronto: Be sure to do it the authentic way, poured over a sugar cube in a slotted spoon.

Cantonese mooncake, David's sleek condo, Toronto: It's sweet, savoury and strange all at once. The Mid-Autumn Festival celebration cake comes in the form of rich bites of sweet lotus paste and a salty egg yolk that represents the mighty moon.

A Manhattan from The Campbell at Grand Central Terminal, New York, NY: This is not a rare or exotic inclusion but this Manhattan à la *Sex in the City* gave me hiccups and double vision for three hours, blanking out most of the Alison Moyet concert I apparently attended. There was definitely no sex in the city that night.

Wormwood and black walnut tea, Kenny's Health Foods, Brantford, ON: It's only fitting that I include this infused tea that is touted for stripping parasites from intestines. It's herbaceous, oddly aromatic and tastes like a sucker punch of grapefruit peels, bad breath and stale root cellar. It was used in absinthe production and was considered hallucinogenic and poisonous. The United States banned it for nearly a hundred years. It didn't cure me of my jungle parasites but it was worth a go.

To Do / To Eat / To Drink
(a.k.a.: my version of a five-year plan)

Cucamelons (Google these. They look like tiny watermelons!)

Gefilte fish

Grandma's dandelion wine, as per the top-secret recipe that I have a copy of.

High tea at the Fairmont Empress Hotel, Victoria, BC

Make "cowboy candy" (candied jalapenos). Better yet, suggest someone else make it (for example, with a subtle hint: a cherished friend like PJ Moore or Cathy Lombard).

Chinese century egg (Not to be confused with a long-lost Cadbury Easter Crème egg. A duck, quail or chicken egg is preserved in a mixture of clay, ash and quicklime for a few months – not one hundred years. The yolk and egg white turns coal black and cola-coloured, like a strange geode.)

Mexican fried ice cream

Butter tea (preferably in Nepal, but not atop Everest)

Coca leaves in Bolivia (preferably without the altitude sickness headache that it's associated with)

Braai on the beach, South Africa, with a 2018 Eekhoring Rooi red

A McDonald's Shamrock shake

Burger King's black-bun Halloween Whopper

Sourtoe cocktail, Dawson, City, Yukon: "You can drink it fast, you can drink it slow – but the lips have gotta touch the toe."

Chef Christina Tossi's Milk Bar Compost Cookie®. The ingredient list reminds me of the pint-sized contestants' creations on *Just Like Mom*. Tossi's cookie is a combo of pretzel bits, potato chips, coffee, oats, graham crackers, chocolate chips and butterscotch.

Chef Tossi's Cereal Milk™ soft-serve made with cornflakes, brown sugar, milk and a pinch of salt. It's supposed to be reminiscent of the last glugs of milk in the bottom of a bowl of cornflakes.

Turkey dressing poutine, Stoyles Fish & Chips, Cambridge, ON (Update: Stoyles closed on May 1, 2021, after 54 years of operation. This poutine will have to be the first listing on my Extinct Food List. Sigh.)

A proper clambake, Cabbage Island, Boothbay Harbour, Maine

A flying fish sandwich, Bequia, Grenadines (because my sister said so)

Kava in Vanuatu (inspired by J. Maarten Troost's *Getting Stoned with Savages: A Trip Through the Islands of Fiji and Vanuatu*)

Charcoal ice cream, Bangkok, Thailand (I didn't have the appetite for it after a day of barfing up in-flight congee post-flight from Beijing.)

Pawpaw (They are supposed to taste like a mango that kissed a banana.)

Pink grapefruit margaritas at The Diplomat Boutique Hotel in Mérida, Mexico (because I promised our friends who own it that we would come visit more than seven years ago)

Snake wine, Vietnam (rice wine bottled with a venomous snake – *hoan hô!*)

One of those overpriced field-to-fork, forest-to-plate kind of events where you drop two hundred bucks and walk around a field or forest visiting stations manned by top chefs serving bites of pine needle foam on birchbark-wrapped truffles sniffed out by a truffle pig. Or something to that effect.

Disclaimer

At forty-six, there are some things that I won't try based on gut reaction, morals and molars. Twenty years ago, before my street vendor-induced bouts of E. coli and follow-up shitting-my-pants episodes in Ecuador, Belize, Colombia and Uganda, I would have voluntarily eaten anything from bat soup to lizard-on-a-stick to battered tarantulas with a side of fries. They say never say never, but now that I am so sage and weary of diarrhea (especially in countries with pit toilets), I will never eat/drink the following:

- bird's nest soup
- shark fin soup
- foie gras (with a confession that I've had it once and loved it but felt too terrible about it to repeat)
- horse, dog, turtle, kangaroo, veal, snails, lizard, bat

- Fettucine alfredo
- Baileys Red Velvet Cream Liqueur
- Coors Light (*exception: pure survival reasons)

Top Ten Leftovers

A bunch of stuff that is still good but doesn't really go with the other stuff. Here are some day-old facts and random info about Brooke Shields, Juicy Fruit gum wrapper chains and rattlesnakes.

1. Little Mikey, who enthusiastically ate Life cereal in a 1972 commercial, was still eating it twelve years later. It was one of the longest continuous commercial campaigns, filmed with his real-life brothers. "Let's get Mikey! He hates everything!"

2. My pal Antoine Von Baich, who I was supposed to go break and bake bread with in Australia, did exactly that. With his older bro, Georg, the duo opened Loafer Bread in Melbourne. The boys paid homage to their mother who ground her own flour and carried on the tradition. Their Australian rye flour loaves were mixed with sprouted grains and ethically sourced ingredients. Andrea Brabazon purchased Loafer

Bread in 2007, with a promise to uphold the Von Baich ethos.

3. Kaitlin Simoes, who always begged me to sign up for a cake decorating course with her, opened The Polly Fox Bakery and Bistro in Abbotsford, British Columbia. The Fraser Valley bakery makes gluten-free, peanut-free, worry-free baked goods like maple-glazed vegan apple fritters "fried into dreamy little pillows of yum" and Keto Bombs pumped with feel-good coconut butter and maca root powder, sweetened with monk fruit.

4. There are custom scratch-and-sniff sticker companies that will create bespoke DIY promotional stickers for you these days. The scents are guaranteed to last a year (as my Grandma always said, things used to be built to last) and the scratch-release spot varnish can be customized to any size or shape for marketing materials. The scent catalogue is a giant leap from the dill pickle and root beer stickers of my youth. Now you can order stickers that smell like sausage, Mexican food, marijuana, campfire, new car, suntan oil and durian.

5. Speaking of smelly things, remember Grapple® apples? The kid-friendly marketing ploy bathes Washington Gala or Fuji apples in a solution of artificial grape flavouring and water. The end result is an apple that smells like grape juice, which is apparently more tempting to the average child.

6. Aunt Jemima's pancake mix and syrup was rebranded as Pearl Milling Company in June 2021 after a push to abolish the original racial stereotype and logo. Nancy Green, a former slave, became the face of the product in 1890. Black Lives Matter protests inspired the change and led others, like Uncle Ben's, to follow suit.

7. In 1995, Brooke Shield's famously "tied the knot" during an episode of *The Jay Leno Show*. This tongue-tying ability supposedly (according to bar rumours) suggests that the individual is a great kisser due to their tongue dexterity.

8. In January 2020, Gary Michael Duschl established the Guinness World Record for creating the longest bubble gum wrapper chain in the world. His unexpected work-in-progress began in 1965 and is twenty miles (106,810 feet) long and contains a total of 2,583,335 Wrigley's Juicy Fruit, Doublemint, Spearmint, Winterfresh and Big Red wrappers. In a 2020 *New York Post* article, he explained how, in the 1960s, "gum wrapper chains were a fad. Girls and boys would make a chain the length matching their boyfriend or girlfriend's height," he said. Per tradition, he has tied together 5.3 feet of chain per day, "which is the length of my wife."

9. In 2001, my dad and brother accidentally ate rattlesnake at a Buffalo Bills tailgate buffet event. I'm still not sure which is more unlikely: my dad eating snake or my brother attending a football game. Regardless, my dad insisted, "It tasted just like chicken!"

10. You can make really remarkable cookies using boxed cake mix in just nine minutes. You add two eggs and a third of a cup of vegetable oil to a box of cake mix and the magic naturally unfolds. Google "Cake Mix Fudge Crinkle Cookies" for proof.

Ten Pro Tips Gleaned from My Mother

1. Invest in a professional whipped cream dispenser and N20 cream chargers. N20 is a colourless and tasteless gas used to magically flip and whip whipping cream (36 percent) or double cream (48 percent) into whipped cream suitable for French toast, tiramisu, crepes or __. Dax latched her onto this gadget and somehow my mother has been able to work whipped cream into every meal from breakfast to midnight snack.

2. Use panettone, an Italian sweet bread easily found at Christmas, for French toast.

3. Fry your French toast and/or panettone in bacon fat (or else). There's no point otherwise.

4. Invert whatever sweet thing you are eating to capitalize on the flavour profiles that are generally found on the top of a cupcake or square. Your taste bud intake will increase tenfold, versus the very best part touching only the roof of your

mouth. It's like practising Kama Sutra at the dinner table.

5. Never, ever substitute applesauce or avocado for butter or oil to make a lower-fat version of a dessert. Abomination! (Kim's mother was the polar opposite in her approach.)

6. Whenever possible, use full-fat milk, cream and sour cream.

7. Double the sugar and don't be afraid to turn an ordinary banana or zucchini loaf into a chocolate one.

8. Buy a Silpat non-stick baking pad. The silicone and fibreglass sheets don't require greasing and your cookies will be perfect every time. Another grateful nod to Dax and his test kitchen!

9. At any holiday gathering, be sure to use every dish and serving platter in your cupboards because as the head cook, you will be relieved from dishwashing duty and will buy two hours of down time that can be spent drinking the latest Portuguese vinho verde.

10. Dark chocolate, always.

Suggested Reading

French Milk by Lucy Knisley – Knisley illustrates a sometimes trying but always delicious month-long romp with her mother through Paris via words and doodles.

A Fork in the Road: Tales of Food and Travel by Anik See – The mash-up of See's roadie tales through places like Patagonia, Iran and Java by foot and bike is punctuated by recipes with props from James Barber. Neat fact: See was the gofer on Barber's *The Urban Peasant* set.

Apron Strings: Navigating Food and Family in France, Italy, and China by Jan Wong – Wong's savoury and saucy account of travels with her twenty-two-year-old son is laced with history, tradition and curiosity. From Grenache to Gorgonzola, polenta to cannoli, Wong guides hungry readers through the pantries, paddocks and woks behind iconic dishes.

Feeding My Mother: Comfort and Laughter in the Kitchen as My Mom Lives with Memory Loss by Jann Arden – Be prepared to have your heart squashed in an emotional panini press. Heartbreakingly honest with Arden's signature ability to make fans laugh and cry in the same breath, this memoir is a gorgeous tribute to her mother and the unspoken love communicated through cooking.

An Embarrassment of Mangoes: A Caribbean Interlude by Ann Vanderhoof – In this memoir, Ann and her husband decide to jump ship on their hectic Toronto lives in favour of a 42-foot sailboat and two-year voyage. It's the stuff of fantasy – Ann and Steve quit their jobs and rent out their house to navigate and nibble on forty-seven islands. It's a rum- and sun-soaked sail with interspersed Carib recipes that promise to bring the equator right into your kitchen.

Kitchen Confidential: Adventures in the Culinary Underbelly by Anthony Bourdain – Bourdain split open the restaurant industry like an oyster with this one. If you've ever wondered what goes on behind closed doors, he lays it all out buffet-style. It's sex, drugs, rock 'n' roll with frank PSA's like when not to order fish.

The Particular Sadness of Lemon Cake by Aimee Bender – Nine-year-old Rose Edelstein bites off more than she can chew when she realizes that she has the ability to detect emotions with her elevated taste buds. The fictional story is pure magic and gives pause: Can we taste feelings? Would it be a gift or a curse?

The Alice B. Toklas Cook Book by Alice B. Toklas – Toklas paints a bleak yet colourful time between wars in Paris, France. Food rations eliminated milk and butter from their diets – a single egg was so precious. Coffee was gold dust. However, Toklas manages bouillabaisse and boeuf bourguignon and other French classics to keep her companion, Gertrude Stein, and notables like Picasso and Hemingway, satiated.

A Kitchen Safari: Stories & Recipes from the African Wilderness by Yvonne Short and Dumi Ndlovu – This book is a 192-page daydream. The safari circumnavigates Africa, including Côte d'Ivoire, Cairo and Zanzibar, with visits to the most stunning game reserves and lodges en route. From smoked springbok carpaccio to spiced orange ice cream, your mind will drift.

Stuffed: Adventures of a Restaurant Family by Patricia Volk – Members of Volk's Jewish-American family tree have been feeding New Yorkers for more than a century. Her great-grandfather introduced pastrami to America back in 1888. Those who gather at the Volk dining table live lives as full as their stomachs and make for an entertaining guest list to eavesdrop on.

Garlic & Sapphires: The Secret Life of a Critic in Disguise by Ruth Reichl – Reichl is the former editor-in-chief of *Gourmet* magazine. She knows her stuff and any resto she strides into quivers a little. Her behind-the-scenes expose the high-lights of some of her disguises and identities over the years, and the change in service that they dictated.

County Heirlooms: Recipes and Reflections from Prince Edward County by Natalie Wollenberg and Leigh Nash – It's like mingling at a cocktail party whose invite list includes only the coolest movers and shakers from the county. Meet the farmers, butchers, breweries and visionaries behind Ontario's pocket of culinary gold.

Julie and Julia: My Year of Cooking Dangerously by Julie Powell – It's impossible not to cheerlead Powell's attempts at cooking all 524 recipes in Julia Child's *Mastering the Art of French Cooking* in one year – and blog about it in tandem. It's ambitious, agonizing and a triumph – and includes more butter than I've bought in a lifetime.

How to Eat Fried Worms by Thomas Rockwell – After yet another book rejection, Rockwell was inspired by the lyrics, "Nobody likes me, every-one hates me, guess I'll go eat worms." This 1973 classic is timeless. Neat fact: Thomas is the son of Norman Rockwell (yes, *that* Norman!).

How to Eat a Fried Worm: An Exclusive Recipe

Ingredients
- 1 dew worm
- 1 small free-range egg, beaten
- ¼ cup of flour
- ½ cup of panko
- Freshly ground Lampung pepper from Indonesia
- Juniper smoked sea salt from the Newfoundland Salt Company, to taste
- 1 tablespoon Frank's Original RedHot Buffalo Wings Hot Sauce
- 2 tablespoons Hellman's mayonnaise
- 2 tablespoons olive oil
- One lime, quartered
- Paper towel
- Wax paper

Instructions
– Pat dew worm dry with a paper towel to remove dew.
– Season liberally with ground pepper and salt.
– Dip worm into flour, shake off excess.
– Dip worm lightly in beaten egg to coat. Let excess drip off.
– Dredge worm in panko, pressing worm into bread crumbs.
– Lay worm on piece of wax paper.
– Heat a small skillet over medium heat. Add oil.
– Lay worm in pan, until it begins to brown (about two minutes).
– Turn and cook until equally brown on the other side (about two minutes).

Dip
Mix mayonnaise and Frank's together until blended.

Serve panko-crusted fried worm with Frank's Hot Sauce, mayo and quartered lime.

Suggested pairing
Early Bird Cold Brew Milk Stout from Coronado Brewing Co., San Diego. Because the early bird gets the worm.

About the Author

Jules Torti is the former editor-in-chief of *Harrow-smith* magazine. She has been published in *The Vancouver Sun*, *The Globe and Mail*, *Canadian Running*, *Cottage Life* and *Massage Therapy Canada*. After looking at 88 houses and living in a barn for a year, she unexpectedly found her home on the 45th parallel: halfway to the North Pole and better yet, halfway to the equator. She lives with her wife on the Saugeen Peninsula in Lion's Head, Ontario. She is the author of *Free to a Good Home: With Room for Improvement* (Caitlin Press) and *Trail Mix: 920 km on the Camino de Santiago* (Rocky Mountain Books). She is now the Communications Architect at Wild Women Expeditions. Despite outward appearances and an affection for kale and 12-grain things, Torti still believes that strawberry Pop-Tarts make for a well-balanced meal (and day).